CHESTERTON *is* EVERYWHERE

David Fagerberg

CHESTERTON *is* EVERYWHERE

David Fagerberg

EMMAUS
ROAD
PUBLISHING

Steubenville, Ohio
A Division of Catholics United for the Faith
www.emmausroad.org

Emmaus Road Publishing
827 North Fourth Street
Steubenville, Ohio 43952

Library of Congress Control Number :2013945034

ISBN: 978-1-937155-14-8

Front cover design and illustrations by Theodore Schluenderfritz
Layout and design by Theresa Westling

To Msgr. Michael Heintz
One of the few people I know whose wit and
wisdom can match Chesterton's.

A convert is grateful to the Catholics who
met him at the border, but he is even more grateful
to the guide who brings him further inland.

Table of Contents

PART 4
Catholicism

PART 5
Transcendent Truths

FOREWORD

He may even have waved his hand in a dismissive gesture, my friend, when he explained his dislike of Chesterton. "It's all rhetoric," he said, and his voice by itself comprehensively dismissed Chesterton as a writer one should read even if he didn't add a backhanded wave of his hand. He meant by *rhetoric* what others would have called "word games" and "verbal fireworks" or even "hot air": an effect without meaning, and a seductive effect at that— seductive, at least, for those easily moved by clever language or looking for cheap debating points.

This left me bemused, partly because my friend was a biblical scholar and therefore someone trained in the careful analysis of language. He spent his life reading the Scriptures and figuring out what the writers were trying to say partly by how they said it, and separating the expression of the writer's mind and personality from the intended effect. Here, he would say, St. Paul struggled to convey a subtle insight and wound up writing very complicated sentences to try to get the meaning down precisely, there he quoted a hymn that his hearers would know, perhaps to bolster the authority of what he was telling them, and there he alluded to a passage from the Scriptures to connect this established idea with the new twist he was giving it.

I would have thought my friend would have seen what Chesterton was doing in writing the way he did, seen that sometimes the "rhetoric" just expressed the way the man thought and sometimes it was a way to make a point to people not always inclined to accept it or even give it a hearing. But my friend, for various reasons, didn't. I felt like a young man told his fiancé was just a pretty face, with the implication that were he wiser he would have seen this and proposed to someone else. Switching the subject seemed the only thing to do.

His response bemused me for another reason. Like the young man engaged to a woman both pretty and virtuous whose friends assume that because she's beautiful she can't be virtuous, when he is more taken by her virtue than her beauty, I had found in reading G. K. Chesterton someone who saw deeply, who showed me truths I had not seen or had not seen clearly. That he wrote entertainingly was a bonus, as if liver tasted like filet mignon. Yet my friend, and several people I read, assumed that if he was fun to read (and some of them didn't think he was all that much fun to read) he couldn't be insightful.

When I started reading Chesterton, I discovered someone who showered insights the way someone sowing grass by hand throws seeds, constantly, profligately, in great handfuls. He was fun to read but had he been much less enjoyable I would have devoured his writing anyway. Insight by itself excites. Truth well put gives pleasure.

David Fagerberg has clearly had the same experience, and it began in the same way as mine. He also picked up a Chesterton book for partly financial reasons, he (as he explains in his introduction) to spend all the money he'd budgeted for that trip to the bookstore (and what reader does not understand this reasoning?), I because the book was so cheap at the book sale that it would be irresponsible to leave such a book unbought (and what reader does not understand this reasoning as well?).

We'd both heard good things of Chesterton but not read him, and neither of us (if I read correctly between David's lines) had placed him high among the authors we must read. We both started reading him with disappointment, he puzzled by the beginning of *Orthodoxy*, I completely baffled by the entire book *St. Francis*. But we did not give up. David was "intrigued" by the chapter of *Orthodoxy* titled "The Suicide of Thought" and then pleased, indeed clearly hooked, by the later one titled "The Ethics of Elfland." I stumbled across his late book *The Thing: Why I Am a Catholic* and loved his explanation of the truths the Catholic Church sees that the Protestant alternatives do not. It strikes me now as at many points unfair to Protestantism, I admit, but it led me to other things.

In both our cases, the discovery that here was a man well worth reading and indeed a writer high among the authors we must read has led to years of pleasure and learning. For me, and I suspect for David, in Chesterton I discovered a man who told me truths I needed to know. These truths were of two sorts: truths I did not see at all or truths I only intuited. In reading him I kept saying "Aha" or "So *that's* it" when he showed me something I had not seen, and "Yes" and "Exactly" when he showed me clearly something I'd only seen dimly or in a glass darkly. Many of the truths Chesterton taught me (truths of both sorts) in my first couple of decades reading him were truths about the Catholic Church and faith to which I found myself drawn but thought at the time I could not possibly enter.

As an example of the first kind of insight, there was Chesterton's line from *The Catholic Church and Conversion* that "We do not really want a religion that is right where we are right. We want a religion that is right where we are wrong." Well, yes, *obviously*, readers may be thinking. But a Protestant attracted to the Catholic Church, at least a theologically-minded one, tends to come to her with a list of commitments the Catholic Church must satisfy. We are thinking about changing our fundamental religious identity but only if we can keep much of what we already hold. The Church has to be right where we are (we think) right. We look at the Church the way a man looks at a job offer when he's fairly satisfied with the job he has and thinks the new job looks like a lateral move.

I looked at the Church like that, anyway. And then reading through Chesterton's short book, I hit this one line and stopped short. I might have said that I wanted a Church that was right where I was wrong, but I was sure I was right about the commitments the Church must satisfy. I just wasn't sure in which religious body I should hold them. On that, I would have said, the Church might be right where I was wrong, but she must be right where I was right on everything else.

But Chesterton's insight, so simply but pungently put, stopped me short. I think it was the contrast between the sentences, the first setting me up and the second knocking me down. Certainly the effect of having read so much Chesterton helped as well, because I knew and trusted the man and because I'd seen the way he came to this insight. I suddenly realized that I wanted a Church that was right where I was wrong and that I might be wrong, absolutely and completely wrong, about a great many things I thought I had down cold. I saw that I might just not be wrong on particular points but that I might be seeing the whole thing the wrong way round. I might need, as people say nowadays, a radical paradigm shift.

As an example of the second kind of insight, when Chesterton showed me clearly something I'd only vaguely understood, there was his famous line, "If a thing's worth doing, it's worth doing badly" from *What's Wrong With the World*. I'd heard it before, I'm sure, it being one of those lines lots of people quote (the second item a web search for the phrase brought up was a column from *Psychology Today*) and thought it was silly. Why do anything if you can't do it well, I thought. The line seemed to me what my friend had dismissed as "rhetoric."

But I was an unconscious Aristotelian and would-be Thomist, in the senses Chesterton explained so well in *The Dumb Ox*. And I believed, or wanted to believe, in the goodness of the world as I found it—I wanted to believe, as I only saw much later, that the world as I found it had been created and created by someone who being good had made it good. I sensed all this but almost everything I had been taught—that the world was just here, the product of no one's mind or intention, with all that implies about human action and responsibility—prevented me from seeing it clearly.

Again Chesterton's insight, so simply but pungently put, stopped me short. Here I think the effect was in the surprise at the end, that "badly," which made me look again at the beginning, the "thing worth doing" and thus at my understanding of things in general. I would have seen a more philosophical statement of the matter as something to be analyzed. And again the insight gained effect because I knew and trusted the man and assumed he meant something worth reflecting upon and because the book I'd been reading led me to see the truth of what he'd put in a few words. I saw, with the deep pleasure of someone who has suddenly grasped something he'd never been able to get his hands around, that the world was a good place, a fundamentally good place.

I could offer several more examples. One learns facts and techniques and methods and insights from many writers, and from some one learns a great deal. But few writers, I think, have Chesterton's transformative effect, at least upon readers like David Fagerberg and me. (Why he leaves some very intelligent people cold is a mystery, like why some people don't like, say, bitter ale. It's a fallen world and some good things are open to some of us and closed to others.) Often, as with these two quotes, his insights seem obvious—*after* you see them. But even after you see them, it is hard to think of a better way of stating them. They are insights you go back to.

Hence the value of this book. *Chesterton Is Everywhere* offers an extended exercise in drawing out Chesterton's insights on a very, very wide number of subjects, from someone who clearly has found many of them mind- and even life-changing. And drawn out, I should add, by a thoughtful man who has read a lot of Chesterton and a lot of other people, and has thought carefully about the world, and therefore offers insights to the long-time reader of Chesterton as well as the new one. Bravo.

David Mills
Executive Editor, *First Things*

INTRODUCTION

The way this collection of essays came to be is a fairly straightforward story. I found Chesterton quite by accident: I added a $2.50 copy of *Orthodoxy* to an armful of books to bring my total exactly up to my spending limit on that visit. Like most people, I had heard Chesterton's name in association with a clever quotation, but knew nothing more about him. When I finally cracked the book, the chapter on "The Maniac" puzzled me; the chapter on "The Suicide of Thought" intrigued me; but the chapter on "The Ethics of Elfland" put a grin on my face that has been there ever since. I read some more. I gathered up my favorite theological quotes intending to write an article, but I found so many favorite quotes that I sorted them into different computer files, and then each file became a chapter in my book *The Size of Chesterton's Catholicism* (so I tell my students that the book is an article with a glandular problem). The editors of *Gilbert* noted the book's appearance, and asked me if I had any scraps on the cutting room floor. Indeed I had. Finally, after a few contributions as a guest, they invited me to be a regular contributor, and it has been my pleasure to produce eight essays per year. Most of them have their origin in a faint smile caused by an irony, a juxtaposition, a curiosity, a foolishness, a forgiveness. Something connects in my mind with a Chestertonian point of view. These essays do not so much look at Chesterton, as they use Chesterton to look at things.

But that is the point: Chesterton is everywhere! His work is designed for daily life, not for the shelves of an academic's library. I am always amazed at how relevant his words from a century ago are today, as if he were wandering Times Square in New York instead of Fleet Street in London. Most especially, he had the capacity to see the practical results that will come out of a thought, like a man who could look at an acorn and see the oak. Chesterton analyzes the nose of the camel before it can come completely under the tent. That is why I think it is worthwhile to recover Chesterton in our own day. He wrote, "If some small mistake were made in doctrine, huge blunders might be made in human happiness."

I have taken these essays out of their chronological order of appearance, and organized them around five themes.

Part 1 concerns the key to a commodity desperately missed by our time: happiness. Chesterton called this key "the doctrine of conditional joy," in other words, the teaching that happiness comes at a cost. To attain happiness we need more than a mood, we need a creed.

Part 2 concerns the ordinary. Chesterton defended the common life of ordinary people because Chesterton said of himself that "I am ordinary in the correct sense of the term; which means the acceptance of an order; a Creator and the Creation, the common sense of gratitude for Creation, life and love as gifts permanently good, marriage and chivalry as laws rightly controlling them, and the rest of the normal traditions of our race and religion." Against the creeping prejudice that the real action is in the workplace, the marketplace, the entertainment industry, Chesterton finds more expansive freedom and eternal adventure in the home. He calls it "the thrill of domesticity."

Part 3 samples some of Chesterton's comments on social reform. He is not easy to pin down on the typical political landscape. He said, "The whole modern world has divided itself into Conservatives and Progressives. The business of Progressives is to go on making mistakes. The business of the Conservatives is to prevent the mistakes from being corrected." Since he wishes to both cease making mistakes and to correct the ones that have been made, we are not able to shelve him in one camp or the other. His most valuable gift is his annoying habit of making us pause to ask what our principles are, and what our end shall be when we make social reform. It is a source of immense satisfaction to me that when I teach Chesterton as an elective to undergraduates at the University of Notre Dame, they tell me that "he has taught me how to think."

Part 4 explores Chesterton's apologetics. In the modern spirit of disclosure, which is assumed to somehow validate an author, I will make the confession that Chesterton was the single most influential person to bring me into the Catholic Church. Like him, I am not a cradle Catholic but a credo Catholic, who entered the Church as an adult after rational investigation. Here there are essays on festivals and feasts, doctrine and liberty, faith and hope. Chesterton laughed about having backed into Catholicism. "It may be, Heaven forgive me, that I did try to be original; but I only succeeded in inventing all by myself an inferior copy of the existing traditions of civilized religion. . . . I did try to found a heresy of my own; and when I had put the last touches to it, I discovered that it was orthodoxy."

Part 5 is included as a reminder that Chesterton is not speaking to the Catholic club, he is speaking about the transcendent truths that weigh upon every human being. Chesterton called the Catholic Church "the trysting-place of all the truths in the world," and in this part some of those rules for life are explored.

I apologize to the reader for failing to do justice to Chesterton's wit and style. The book will justify itself if it leads the reader to seek out something by the master himself; here I am repaying a debt to my friend, Gilbert Chesterton.

PART 1
Happiness

*"Existence often ceases to be beautiful;
but if we are men at all it never ceases to be interesting."*
December 6, 1905

EN-JOY!

Chesterton was so clamorously happy that it is still infectious from a distance of six decades. This helps explain why those bitten by the Chesterton bug relapse regularly into his writings. It is not only that his style is often droll (he wrote in his autobiography, "I have never understood . . . why a solid argument is any less solid because you make the illustrations as entertaining as you can"). Or that he can entertain the reader as well as himself (he used to write in a pub on Fleet Street and Maisie Ward records the headwaiter describing him thus: "'Your friend,' he whispered, admiringly, 'he very clever man. He sit and laugh. And then he write. And then he laugh at what he write'"). It is most of all Chesterton's confidence that happiness is the proper end of every human person, as affirmed by the Church he finally entered. "For Catholics it is a fundamental dogma of the Faith that all human beings, without any exception whatever, were specially made, were shaped and pointed like shining arrows, for the end of hitting the mark of Beatitude."

I would like to consider the nature of Chesterton's beatitude, because it seems to me, from his writings, that he has a different concept of happiness than mere enjoyment. In fact, enjoyment can stifle happiness. "The pagan set out, with admirable sense, to enjoy himself. By the end of his civilization he had discovered that a man cannot enjoy himself and continue to enjoy anything else." The prefix "en-" usually means "in, into," as en-danger means to put in danger, and en-gender means to put into existence. To en-joy should therefore mean to instill joy (children en-joy their parents), but we have reversed the current and use the word to describe the feeling caused by an object (children enjoy their toys). We have turned its active sense (*enjoie* meant to give joy to) into a passive sense. We have done the same with the word "love," by the way. The French philosopher Gustav Thibon roots the word in the Latin *lubere, libere* which mean, successively, "to please" and "to liberate." If that were the case, to love someone would not be feeling ticklish feelings when he or she is around, it would be serving, caring for, tending to, pleasing, and meeting that person's needs. Love is a work. Chesterton observes this very point about married love. "In everything worth having, even in every pleasure, there is a point of pain or tedium that must be survived, so that the pleasure may revive and endure. . . . If a man is bored in the first five minutes he must go on and force himself to be happy." Surely, then, by happiness Chesterton does not mean the fleeting feelings of bliss. The word beatitude comes from *beatus* (happy), but it has roots in *beare* (to bless), which is akin to *bonus* (good). For Chesterton, these two later meanings seem somehow folded into the first.

One can refresh the word "happiness" by recalling that the word's root, "hap," does also exist in the English language, although it is hardly ever used. It means a person's luck or lot, so we speak of a "hapless child." It means an occurrence or accident, so we say "something happened." The dictionary informs me that it comes from *gehaep,* meaning suitable, so we say "that table was a happy choice." This does not mean the subject felt happy making the choice, nor that the table felt happy for having been chosen, it only means the table is suitable, it belongs, it fits the space well. Happily.

With this in mind, we can get nearer Chesterton's understanding of happiness by stating the very true fact, but not so obvious a fact, and a fact denied by many modern philosophies, that one can make oneself happy. One can make oneself well-fitted to a person, a cause, or a task—indeed, one can make oneself ultimately happy by becoming well-fitted to ultimate reality. "Man cannot love mortal things. He can only love immortal things for an instant. . . . Ultimately a man cannot rejoice in anything except the nature of things. Ultimately a man can enjoy nothing except religion." Nothing finite will be finally suitable for our infinite longing, which is another way of saying nothing finite will finally make us happy.

To make oneself happy in this sense would, of course, require knowing the real nature of the world. The way to this knowledge would be through what Chesterton called his doctrine of conditional joy, which states that "an incomprehensible happiness rests upon an incomprehensible condition." In two of his more laconic descriptions of the doctrine he writes, "we should thank God for beer and Burgundy by not drinking too much of them," and "keeping to one woman is a small price for so much as seeing one woman." Were we to succeed in this self-ordering, then we would find that all things in the world also have their order—they would be happy things. In a letter to Frances, after confessing his hands were stained from the pen, he thinks to write, "I like the Cyclostyle ink; it is so inky. I do not think there is anyone who takes quite such fierce pleasure in things being themselves as I do. The startling wetness of water excites and intoxicates me; the fieriness of fire, the steeliness of steel, the unutterable muddiness of mud. It is just the same with people. . . . When we call a man 'manly' or a woman 'womanly' we touch the deepest philosophy."

Chesterton's is a happy voice. It is both a cheerful, gladsome voice, and a voice which is just what our time needs. He points out that sometimes en-joying a person is a work, a labor, an active state and not a passive one. He believes our glory lies in becoming happy, or suitable for God. We are beings who become, and we can make ourselves into just the stone that precisely fits this niche in God's temple or exactly the word God needs in this stanza of the cosmic poem he is composing. While in the world, we can love immortal things for the brief moment they are in existence. Chesterton's doctrine of conditional joy understands this world to be a place where one can train for beatitude.

THE FASHIONABLE
MR. CHESTERTON

People turn admiringly to Chesterton for a great many reasons: for his sense of humor, his sense of rhetorical style, his sense of distributist justice. Few people, however, turn to Chesterton for his fashion sense, like I do.

Gilbert magazine often carries a photo in its pages of a rumpled, caped figure under a crushed hat who must have caused smiles among the more fastidious clothiers of London. Chesterton was no fop. I have commented before on the recognition Frances deserves for putting up with Gilbert's casual lack of concern in this area. "Very early in their engagement," records Ward's biography, "she began her own abortive attempts to make him brush his hair, tie his tie straight and avoid made-up ones, attend to the buttons on his coat, and all the rest. It would seem that for a time at any rate he made some efforts, but evidently simply regarded the whole thing as one huge joke." Gilbert's amusement is revealed in this courtship letter:

> My appearance, as I have suggested, is singularly exemplary. My boots are placed, after the fastidious London fashion, on the feet: the laces are done up, the watch is going, the hair is brushed, the sleeve-links are inserted, for of such is the Kingdom of Heaven. As for my straw hat, I put it on eighteen times consecutively, taking a run and a jump to each try, till at last I hit the right angle. I have not taken it off for three days and nights lest I should disturb that exquisite pose. Ladies, princes, queens, ecclesiastical processions go by in vain: I do not remove it. That angle of the hat is something to mount guard over. As Swinburne says—"Not twice on earth do the gods do this."

I liked Chesterton's style the moment I read that passage because I share his attitude toward the modern style of costuming, for which I am in a constant and sincere state of apology to my wife. *Gilbert* magazine usually carries a photo at the top of page forty-two of a bearded gent usually in need of a trim, always lacking a tie, and regularly in want of socks for his sandals. This photo was not snapped one Saturday morning as I prepared to mow the lawn in haste lest the neighbors see me in such disarray; it was snapped in my office between classes. It is not that I intend to disrespect anyone by meeting them in this state—if it would help, I would bow, salute, genuflect, or extend some other ceremonious honor—it is only that I fail to see the symbolic meaningfulness of a limp string of cloth hung round the neck. If adding irrelevant pieces of cloth to one's body is a gesture of honor, then why can I not dress up by adding socks to my feet, something I willingly do when the occasion calls for it? Why is putting a silk rope around one's neck (an act our mothers warned us never to do) more acceptable for expressing formality than putting a wool stocking around one's toes?

In the hands of anyone else, such paths of reasoning could be dangerous, but Chesterton and I are harmless, I swear. We are fashion nonconformists, it is true, but we do not mean to bring down modern civilization. Though social iconoclasts, we are social traditionalists; even religious traditionalists, something not apparent to those who think that enjoying the heights of ritual liturgy requires one to also prefer the heights of high fashion. Actually, the two are incomparable.

Chesterton contrasted "conscious ritual," which is comparatively simple, with "unconscious ritual," which is really heavy and complicated. To the surprise of our friends, he believes that he and I would number among the latter camp. "The ritual which is really complex, and many coloured, and elaborate . . . is the ritual which people enact without knowing it," and "consists of plain things like bread and wine and fire, and men falling on their faces." Of such thick ritual is liturgy made. Liturgy is not made of thin, conscious ritual, which consists of "really peculiar, and local, and exceptional, and ingenious things— things like door-mats, and door-knockers, and silk hats, and white ties." And, may I add, socks. The thin, conscious ritual requires constant consciousness because the meanings are arbitrarily assigned.

> To take one instance out of an inevitable hundred: I imagine that Mr. Kensit takes off his hat to a lady; and what can be more solemn and absurd, considered in the abstract, than symbolizing the existence of the other sex by taking off a

portion of your clothing and waving it in the air? This, I repeat, is not a natural and primitive symbol, like fire or food. A man might just as well have to take off his waistcoat to a lady.

Or, may I add, socks. Perhaps I am in a state of continual salute to the fairer sex.

The point is that social iconoclasts can still be theological ritualists because while being inattentive to what is consciously assigned, they might be quite attentive to those unconscious symbols "which belong to a primary human poetry." This might, at any rate, be of comfort to Frances who once sent Gilbert to a speaking engagement with a new suit, only to have him return without it, forgotten under some bed in some hotel room.

GOOD TO BE HERE

With Chesterton's effulgent cheerfulness exhibited time after time in *Gilbert* magazine, readers might wonder if he was capable of a sober thought, a somber thought, even a funereal thought. How would the cheery man react in the face of sorrow and sadness and even death? We all know people whose jovial veneer, when punctured by something grave, turns abruptly from mocking our foibles to sardonic mockery. How did Chesterton react to the serious things of life, like death?

Two letters written to his fiancée Frances upon the death of her sister, Gertrude, may give a clue. In the first Chesterton writes, "I am so glad to hear you say that, in your own words, 'it is good for us to be here'—where you are at present. The same remark, if I remember right, was made on the mountain of the Transfiguration." He proposes that we should repeat Peter's remark "in contemplating every panoramic change in the long Vision we call life . . . 'It is good for us to be here—it is good for us to be here,' repeating itself eternally. And if, after many joys and festivals and frivolities, it should be our fate to have to look on while one of us is, in a most awful sense of the words, 'transfigured before our eyes': shining with the whiteness of death—at least, I think, we cannot easily fancy ourselves wishing not to be at our post. Not I, certainly. It was good for me to be there."

These lines came to mind today as I return from that same place where Frances was: my mother died abruptly, without warning, and I pen these words but a few days after her funeral. It was a post I would not have abandoned, either.

Death is a crucible in which a metaphysic which believes in the utter goodness of being is tested against all others. Only one can be right. Either human beings were made for annihilation, or expiration, or decomposition, or oblivion, or else, as Chesterton says, "all human beings, without any exception whatever, were specially made, were shaped and pointed like shining arrows, for the end of hitting the mark of Beatitude." Remarkable things happen to life on earth when we believe that after death there is happiness, and more happiness, if we would have it.

In the second letter, Gilbert is in the unusual situation of being at a loss for words. For one word, to be precise. He concludes he cannot improve on the choice made by the Psalmist ("Precious in the sight of the Lord is the death of one of his saints.")

> We could not say that Gertrude's death is happy or providential or sweet or even perhaps good. But it is something. "Beautiful" is a good word—but "precious" is the only right word. It is this passionate sense of the value of things: of the richness of the cosmic treasure: the world where every star is a diamond, every leaf an emerald, every drop of a blood a ruby, it is this sense of *preciousness* that *is* really awakened by the death of His saints. Somehow we feel that even their death is a thing of incalculable value and mysterious sweetness: it is awful, tragic, desolating, desperately hard to bear—but still "precious." . . . Forgive the verbosity of one whose trade it is to express the inexpressible.

Forgive the verbosity of one who struggles to apply Chesterton's words. I have written that he found the truth of his faith before he found the faith itself. He found this metaphysic to be true, and good, and beautiful, and then afterward found the faith which warrants it. These letters to Frances were written five years before he wrote *Orthodoxy*, a quarter century before his reception into the Church of Rome, yet he already knew that we are in need of sanctification.

> I cannot help dreaming of some wild fairy-tale in which the whole round cosmos should be a boiling pot, with the flames of Purgatory under it, and that soon I shall have the satisfaction of seeing such a thing as boiled mountains, boiled cities, and a boiled moon and stars. A tremendous picture. Yet I am perfectly happy as usual. After all, why should we object to be boiled? Potatoes, for example, are better boiled than raw—why should we fear to be boiled into new shapes in the cauldron?

In my mother's house there are many rooms filled with many treasures of which we must now dispose. There are pictures, knick-knacks, books, relics, mementos—all souvenirs from different chapters of her life. She dragged these goods behind her over the years because they were dear to her. But when the final call came, she folded up her tent and slipped quietly away, leaving them behind for us to deal with, because she lived at what Hugo Rahner calls "the exact midpoint between heaven and earth." Only at that place can one "accept and lovingly embrace the world as God's handiwork, and, at the same time, toss it aside as a child would toss a toy of which it had wearied, in order to soar upward into the 'blessed seriousness' which is God alone." Chesterton's gaiety did not blind him to this blessed seriousness, and I believe he found his way home to it, too, and I hope my mother looks him up.

CHESTERTON'S 4-H CLUB

We think of joking and seriousness as mutually opposite states, but, really, they can be conjoined in a surprisingly large number of ways. One can be serious about jokes; one can be joking but thought to be serious; one can be serious but taken as a joke. A spoilsport will be serious during a humorous occasion; a flippant person will joke in self-defense during a grave moment; and the person who sees a bigger picture will joke during a serious occasion because he knows an occasion that is much more serious.

This last is what I suppose Thomas More was doing when he replied to Cromwell's last-minute inquiry whether he would change his mind. More replied he had indeed changed his mind: instead of shaving his beard before execution he would keep it so that it might share the fate of his head. Frivolous people make light of serious moments because they cannot rise to the occasion, but Thomas More was not being frivolous. He did lament that he could not reconcile with his King, but he was certain of the eventual reconciliation of his head with his body, so he could quip to the officer helping him up the stairs to the chopping block, "When I come down again, let me shift for myself as well as I can."

There is a common and binding root between the four words, *humus* (earth, soil), *human, humility,* and *humor.* It is almost as though any three must be in play for the fourth to appear. For example, without a sense of finitude, and forgetting that human beings are made of temporal clay, a person will be too full of himself to have a sense of humor. Frivolity can be a sign of secret despair, but healthy humor is a sign of humility which plants two people on a common ground. More's gallows humor was not flippancy; it is irony being appreciated by an eternal spirit secured in clay. And neither is Chesterton flippant when he laughs at a foolishness. His critics sometimes expected more serious treatment from Chesterton, the way the King may have expected more serious treatment from his ex-Chancellor, but neither More nor Chesterton were being insouciant when they joked, and as to why this was not the case we have Chesterton's explanation.

In the first place, Chesterton doesn't believe entertainment to be inherently incompatible with conviction. He does not see why "convictions should look dull or why jokes should be insincere." In *The Autobiography* he confesses to having never understood

> why a solid argument is any less solid because you make the illustrations as entertaining as you can. . . . If you say that two sheep added to two sheep make four sheep, your audience will accept it patiently—like sheep. But if you say it of two monkeys, or two kangaroos, or two sea-green griffins, people will refuse to believe that two and two make four. They seem to imagine that you must have made up the arithmetic, just as you have made up the illustration of the arithmetic. And though they would actually know that what you say is sense, if they thought about it sensibly, they cannot believe that anything decorated by an incidental joke can be sensible. Perhaps it explains why so many successful men are so dull—or why so many dull men are successful.

Even when he makes his point in humorous form, we are to suppose him adamant about that point.

Yet it is one thing to be able to illustrate a point with an amusement, and it is another for a writer to consistently employ buffoonery. Why did Chesterton so consistently mix his message with mirth? Because humor is a sign of the willingness to dialogue. In *An Apology for Buffoons* Chesterton explains that he seeks to be amusing for the simple fact that he does not see "why the audience should listen unless it is more or less amused." He believes speech should be "what some have fancifully supposed the function of speech to be; something addressed by somebody to somebody else. . . . A man who is only amusing himself need not be amusing." The one person in all the world who does not suffer the burden of entertaining is the soliloquist. If, however, one desires true communication, then one must want to be heard, and one gets a better hearing if one's speech has "all the vices and vulgarities attaching to a speech that really is a speech and not a soliloquy." The person who is only talking to himself needn't be amusing. Perhaps that's why so few of us are amusing.

The person who does not care if he is heard, is the person who does not care to dialogue. The person who does not care if he dialogues, corrodes the bonds of conversation with caustic remarks. Chesterton said "It is generally the man who is not ready to argue, who is ready to sneer. That is why, in recent literature, there has been so little argument and so much sneering." Neither More nor Chesterton were caustic. They were polemicists, yes, but their arguments contained humility and humor which continued to the end of their life, and unlike us they did not sneer at any of their opponents. More did not even contemn the King who killed him.

DESTINY'S PURSUIT

I had a professor once, a friend, really, who said that it would be something of an indictment if it could be said at the end of one's life that one was really an unhappy person. This friend, my professor, did not have in mind people who have had their share of ups and downs, or people who have suffered sorrow and the ordinary range of grief and disappointment. He did not mean people who have occasionally grumbled. He meant people who had become a grumble. It would be something of an indictment on such a life to say at its end that the person who lived it had been fundamentally unhappy. To gain the force of his comment you must focus upon the verb he chose: to *indict* is "to accuse of wrongdoing." A person would have done something wrong to himself by turning himself into an unhappy person. It would be like using the best kitchen knife as a screwdriver, or framing a photograph back facing front, or sleeping in the bathroom. It is not the use to which a life should be put.

I still cannot get through two paragraphs of Chesterton without a smile appearing on my face, but that's not what I'm talking about here. I don't mean that Chesterton was funny. There are many funny people who aren't happy, and many happy people who don't have the knack for being funny. Happiness has more gravity than humor alone. And happiness has a different source.

It is a common conjecture, with a long history behind it, that happiness is destined, as if destiny is the source of happiness. This conjecture believes that a destiny steers a person into happiness or unhappiness, as though anyone from the whole world dropped into this particular matrix of circumstances would become happy, or anyone dropped into that particular matrix of circumstances would become unhappy—like it would be the destiny of cloth dropped in water to become wet, or in sand to become dusty. So Chesterton was happy, we are told, because he was dropped into fame, and a circle of London's elite, and a beautiful home at Beaconsfield. We could be happy, we jealously think, if we possessed the celebrity which comes with a regular column, and recourse to the dazzling conversation of the literati, and life as a country squire.

But perhaps the quality of happiness does not reside in a person as the quality of wetness resides in a rag; perhaps happiness is not so passive; perhaps happiness even has the power to influence destiny.

Such is the thesis of a small book entitled *Wisdom and Destiny* written at the turn of the century by a Belgian author and playwright named Maurice Maeterlinck. He does not mean anything so trite as to say good things will come to us if we think happy thoughts; neither is he so foolish to suggest that we are masters of our fate and accident is only an illusion. But he does mean that wise persons know in advance "how events will be received in their soul. The event in itself is pure water that flows from the pitcher of fate, and seldom has it either savour or perfume or colour." As the soul is, so shall the event be received. As the soul is, so will the event become joyous or sad, become tender or hateful, become deadly or quick with life. Imagine, Maeterlinck goes on to tease, if by some blunder destiny had "lured Epicurus, or Marcus Aurelius, or Antoninus Pius into the snares that she laid around Oedipus. . . .Would that noble sovereign's soul have been hopelessly crushed?" The tragic ending to *Hamlet* turns on vengeance and pride and family honor; but could there not have been some other ending? "Let us imagine a sovereign, all-powerful soul— that of Jesus, in Hamlet's place at Elsinore; would the tragedy then have flown on til it reached the four deaths at the end? Is that conceivable?" Certainly, Maeterlinck admits, the empire of destiny can throw up accidents that cannot be influenced. "I acknowledge her might when a wall crashes down on my head, when the storm drives a ship on the rocks, when disease attacks those whom I love; but into man's soul she never will come, uncalled. Hamlet is unhappy because he moves in unnatural darkness."

Were I a more literate person, I would turn now to a series of imaginative speculations about what alternate endings would suggest themselves had the protagonist been Chesterton instead of Hamlet, Oedipus, Marc Antony, Captain Ahab, Ethan Frome, or Holden Caulfield. But as I distrust my abilities in that field, I will leave that to the reader, and also invite you to speculate what alternate ending would suggest itself if you were the protagonist yourself. My point now is that Chesterton's happiness and destiny are linked, but in a way we don't expect. It was not his destiny or fate or circumstance which made him happy; it was his happiness and character and sagacity which influenced his destiny. And this influence comes not from the scheming mind, says Maeterlinck, but from the loving heart. "The true sage is not he who sees, but he who, seeing the furthest, has the deepest love for mankind. He who sees without loving is only straining his eyes in the darkness." Against such a life there can be no indictment.

THE SAINT AND THE ROMANTIC

There is a movement afoot to make Gilbert Chesterton into a saint of the ecclesiastical variety, but I would think it a fact already established that Frances Chesterton was a saint of the popular variety. I mean a saint by popular acclamation, as when people exclaim, "That woman must be a saint." They would have exclaimed it about Frances, as they would exclaim it about most women, for the valiancy exhibited in living with her husband. Frances had to live with Gilbert. She had to live with Gilbert's forgetfulness, generosity, impracticality, and his bounteous, romantic points of view. I do not pity her for this, but I do sympathize with her.

Frances' industrious care of her oversized Peter Pan is well documented. What would Gilbert have done without Frances to administrate his clothes, his cuisine, his calendar, and his coif? It was she, says Maisie Ward, who "by a stroke of genius decided to make him picturesque. The conventional frockcoat worn so unconventionally, the silk hat crowning a mat of hair, disappeared, and a wide-brimmed slouch hat and flowing cloak more appropriately garbed him. This was especially good as he got fatter." That Gilbert's own attitude toward fashion was a bit more combative, he reveals in a letter written during their engagement. "My clothes have rebelled against me. Weary of scorn and neglect, they have all suddenly come to life and they dress me by force every morning. My frockcoat leaps upon me like a lion and hangs on, dragging me down. As I struggle my boots trip me up—and the laces climb up my feet (never missing a hole) like snakes or creepers. At the same moment the celebrated grey tie springs at my throat like a wild cat." And his sense of grooming was certainly unwitting of the effect its failure might have upon the more delicate temperaments walking London's streets. "Does my hair want cutting?" he writes, repeating Frances' question to him from an earlier letter.

> My hair seems pretty happy. You are the only person who seems to have any fixed theory on this. For all I know it may be at that fugitive perfection which has moved you to enthusiasm. Three minutes after this perfection, I understand, a horrible degeneration sets in: the hair becomes too long, the figure disreputable and profligate: and the individual is unrecognized by all his friends. It is he that wants cutting then, not his hair.

But if Frances suffered Gilbert's distracted unsophisticatedness, she must have loved Gilbert's elemental unsophisticatedness, the two together being of one piece. To remove Gilbert's absent-mindedness from his elementary quality would be to remove the hump from the camel: neither animal would be the same. His simplicity made him a romantic. I use the word to indicate a sense of adventure, easily moved to zeal, prepared to answer the grander and more heroic urges within. Their life would be an adventure, of the sort he described in *The Napoleon of Notting Hill*. Like Notting Hill, their home would be sacred turf, and they its Napoleon and Josephine enthroned. On his wedding day he was as absent-minded as ever ("As Gilbert knelt down the price ticket on the sole of one of his new shoes became plainly visible"), and as quixotic as ever: he stopped on the way to the train station "to buy a revolver with cartridges . . . for the defense of his bride against all possible dangers." Ward says his revolver, his knife, and his sword-stick "stood in his mind for freedom, adventure, personal responsibility." I would summarize by saying he liked the element of romance about them.

But Frances' husband was a romantic with a difference. C. S. Lewis' study of the rise of courtly love shows that "French poets in the 11th century, discovered or invented, or were the first to express, that romantic species of passion which English poets were still writing about in the nineteenth." This species of passion was a concoction of adventure, humility, courtesy to the fairer sex, and adultery. The surprising presence of that last numbered characteristic is accounted for by their supposition that courtly love was adventure, heroism, commitment to the lady of the castle, or rescue of the damsel in distress. But "the same woman who was the lady and the 'dearest dread' of her vassals was often little better than a piece of property to her husband. . . . So far from being a natural channel for the new kind of [passionate, romantic] love, marriage was rather the drab background against which that love stood out in all the contrast of its new tenderness and delicacy." Our televised versions of romantic love share the same assumption that romance flees as familiarity, the ordinary, and the domestic set in. The tension between romantic love and marriage eventually becomes a nagging contradiction.

But Gilbert lived with no such contradiction or tension. He found romance increasing with married life, and spilling over to bathe ordinary things in a new light. And so one of the most romantic lines I can remember him writing came from a letter—after getting lost on their honeymoon!—in which he wrote, "I have a wife, a piece of string, a pencil and a knife; what more can any man want on a honeymoon?" But that woman must have been a saint to receive this, her husband's gift of romantic poetry.

WEATHERWISE

I hope I'm not trespassing upon the province of Frank Petta if I open with a joke. At any rate, I hope it meets the standard set on each Lunacy & Letters page. It goes like this. "Question: How can you tell a Norwegian extrovert? Answer: He looks at the toes of *your* shoes while he talks to you."

That is a somewhat delicate joke for me to tell since I am myself of Scandinavian extraction, and it is true that we are a quiet people. That is why, although it is possible to find a Norwegian in politics or in Hollywood, he suffers a severe handicap. Norwegians do not talk much about themselves on the stray chance that they might enjoy it. We generally discourage calling attention to ourselves and are not much for self-disclosure. Like the fundamentalist Baptist who disallowed sex because it might lead to dancing, we disallow boasting in case it leads to self-disclosure.

Chesterton, it might be said, was more at home in his extroversion than I am in mine. He actually sought out human contact, and he actually enjoyed it. He wrote his articles on a table in the pub or against a wall in the street, as if to keep in touch with people, the way tree roots probe downward to stay in touch with groundwater. Maisie Ward quotes several entries from his early Notebook which give a glimpse into this aspect even in his youth.

> Once I found a friend
> "Dear me," I said, "he was made for me."
> But now I find more and more friends
> Who seem to have been made for me
> And more and yet more made for me,

Is it possible we were all made for each other
all over the world?

In a poem entitled "A Man Born on the Earth" he wrote:

Perhaps there has been some mistake
How does he know he has come to the right place?
But when he finds his friends
He knows he has come to the right place.

When imagining a party among friends, he finds it hard to know where to end the guest list. "My great ambition is to give a party at which everybody should meet everybody else and like them very much." The poem entitled "Invitation" runs:

Mr. Gilbert Chesterton
Requests the pleasure
Of humanity's company
To tea on Dec. 25th 1896
Humanity Esq., The Earth, Cosmos E.

Extroversion comes from "extra" (outside) and "vertere" (to turn), and there is something far worse than Scandinavian shyness which can debilitate this power of turning outwards to others. Chesterton was forever peeved at people who would not turn outside their circle, like the theosophist who would not turn to the sausage-seller, the top hat who would not turn to the beer belly, and the puritan who would not extravert to the pagan. Chesterton's democratic tendencies ran so deep that he thought there was a common human nature under our classes and ranks, like there was a common human body under our uniforms and insignias.

But what would an extrovert talk about with a perfect stranger? Even a Norwegian knows the answer to that question: you talk about the weather! A hundred and one conversations begin every day about the weather.

Some scoff at this overture as run of the mill, and would prefer instead to begin every tête-à-tête at the bus stop and supermarket checkout line with an observation about quarks, or Jane Austen, or the evolution of the Sarum Psalter. But Chesterton thinks two strangers can find more common ground in the sky above than they can find in these specialized topics. "There are very deep reasons for talking about the weather, reasons that are delicate as well as deep," he says, and then names three of them. "First of all it is a gesture of primeval worship. The sky must be invoked; and to begin everything with the weather is a sort of pagan way of beginning everything with prayer." Talk about weather recognizes that we are all under a common sky, living from common celestial blessings.

Second, talk about the weather is also an expression of the most elementary idea in politeness, which is equality. "The very word politeness is only the Greek for citizenship. . . . All good manners must obviously begin with the sharing of something in a simple style. Two men should share an umbrella; if they haven't got an umbrella, they should at least share the rain." *Polis* meant city; being polite is an obligation of common citizenship. The rapid conversationalists may not share the same taste in leisure sports, political persuasions, or business management styles, but without an umbrella they do share the same dampness.

Third, talk about the weather is a deep subject because "it begins with the body and with our inevitable bodily brotherhood. All true friendliness begins with fire and food and drink and the recognition of rain or frost. Those who will not *begin* at the bodily end of things are already prigs and may soon be Christian Scientists." We find more in common when we recognize our common elementary state, and we are aware of that elementary state when we suffer the elements.

Chesterton's extroversion might even have brought him to start a conversation with a taciturn Norwegian standing nearby, looking eagerly at the toe tips of this journalist's shoes. And say, how's the weather where you are?

WHEN SACRIFICE GETS EASY

One of the annual rites of passage and most solemn obligations in the world of academics is a conclave known as "The Faculty Workshop" held each fall, where all instructors, lecturers, and professors are huddled together by administrators for two and a half days to prepare for the coming school year. As I am now exactly halfway between Faculty Workshops—a dreadful way of marking time—I find myself retrospecting upon the last palaver. The theme was how to prepare our students for the future. Naturally, great and mighty concerns about the general future were aired, bemoaning the decline in civilized behavior, social values, and attention spans. But the Workshop's specific focus was on the impact of technology upon the future of higher education: technology in the classroom, new learning styles, utilizing the internet, and even long-distance video education and virtual universities. Some of us harumphed over this set of concerns (mostly faculty who are still getting familiar with email), and some of us cheered this set of concerns (mostly faculty who already know how to post a web page and aren't afraid of sending their credit card numbers to Amazon. com). I wondered at the time how Chesterton would react. Would he embrace technology or be suspicious of it? I did not know.

I think I have a clue now, however, standing here at the midpoint of the year, for I have lived one semester's worth of the future about which we prognosticated. And what had the future brought? One of my students was diagnosed by her physician with multiple sclerosis; you know how quickly that terrible disease will act on a twenty-two-year-old body. Another of my students was absent for a week because her mother died unexpectedly. Some have been betrayed by friends, some have suffered depression, others have been tested in still unexpected ways by life. The spouse of one faculty colleague has only recently learned the results of her biopsy, marking the start of therapy, while another has begun a more radical treatment because the healers are running out of options.

In light of having lived some of the future, the questions put so earnestly at the workshop have taken on a different ring. If every faculty office has a PC, will we be kinder people? If Windows 98 integrates an internet browser, will our personal integrity increase? If modem lines connect dorm rooms at a thousand, or a million, or a billion bytes per second, will we talk to each other more, and listen more compassionately to the little human clues we drop about ourselves but no one picks up? If we can capture the entire content of the Louvre on a CD, will my students know beauty when they see it? If every dorm room has access to every printed word in every printed text in every library in the world, will my students know truth when they read it? We were adamantly informed that the future is filled with uncertainty—who knows what computing will look five years from now!—but I have been reminded that at least one thing in the future is certain: our death.

In *What's Wrong with the World* Chesterton repeatedly makes the argument that we cannot create anything good until we have conceived it, and we cannot conceive it until we know for what end a thing should exist. This accounts for his fascination with the medieval world. He does not laud that civilization because he pines for a simpler, ruder folk. He loves it because in that civilization even the simple, rude folk accepted the value of theorizing.

> Suppose a great a commotion arises in the street about something, let us say a lamp-post, which many influential persons desire to pull down. A grey-clad monk, who is the spirit of the Middle Ages, is approached upon the matter, and begins to say, in the arid manner of the Schoolmen, "Let us first of all consider, my brethren, the value of Light. If Light be in itself good"—At this point he is somewhat excusably knocked down. All the people make a rush for the lamp-post, the lamp-post is down in ten minutes, and they go about congratulating each other on their unmedieval practicality. But as things go on they do not work out so easily. Some people have pulled the lamp-post down because they wanted the electric light; some because they wanted old iron; some because they wanted darkness, because their deeds were evil. Some thought it not enough of a lamp-post, some too much; some acted because they wanted

to smash municipal machinery; some because they wanted to smash something. And there is war in the night, no man knowing whom he strikes. So, gradually and inevitably, today, tomorrow, or the next day, there comes back the conviction that the monk was right after all, and that all depends on what is the philosophy of Light. Only what we might have discussed under the gas-lamp, we now must discuss in the dark.

There are easy reasons for opposing technology, from gas lamps to transistor tubes to pentium chips. What Chesterton wants to discuss is the very practical questions, "Are they good? What are they good for?"

Certainly, his theories of distributism will advocate the simple life if complexity proves to be the problem. He opposes the demigods of greed who put into effect "the heresy of altering the human soul to fit its conditions, instead of altering human conditions to fit the human soul." They argue "You cannot have equality in a soap factory; so you cannot have it anywhere. . . . We must have commercial civilization; therefore we must destroy democracy." Chesterton says if the choice be put to him, it will be an easy one. "If soap-boiling is really inconsistent with brotherhood, so much the worst for soap-boiling, not for brotherhood. . . . Certainly, it would be better to do without soap rather than to do without society. Certainly, we would sacrifice all our wires, wheels, systems, specialties, physical science and frenzied finance for one half-hour of happiness such as has often come to us with comrades in a common tavern." It is not difficult to expand his list to include computers, with their mass of tangled cables, right between the wires and wheels he mentions; or the Windows and Mac wars right between the systems and specialties he mentions; or silicon valley and Bill Gates right between physical science and frenzied finance.

It is as easy to credit or blame technology because it is only a tool, and as a tool it amplifies our native power, and we have a power for good and for ill. But Chesterton concludes the above paragraph with the following sentence: "I do not say the sacrifice will be necessary; I only say it will be easy." If soap and the mainframe gets in the way of human fellowship, then so much the worse for soap and IBM. It will be an easy choice—if it becomes necessary! But the computer is only a tool, as is soap. Tools facilitate work. Soap makes getting clean easier; the microscope extends our vision; the lever, the pulley, and the inclined plane augment our strength. Being for or against technology, then, is like being for or against any other tool—soap, a pencil, a hammer, a hydroelectric dam. One can't be for or against the thing; one can, however, pass judgment upon what someone is doing with the thing. The question is what we plan to *do* with the tool, and the answer to that does not lie in the CPU, tucked between its memory chips; it lies in the one who wields the tool. Chesterton does not say a sacrifice will be necessary, only that, if we are properly disposed, it will be easy.

A WILLING PLAYMATE

I wonder if readers of this page will tire of me celebrating Chesterton's festive nature? Is it possible to visit the theme of his cheerfulness too often? Though I myself cannot suppress a yokel's grin when I think of him on his knees to see eye to eye with a child, or hailing a hansom cab for a half-block ride, or his fondness for beer and burgundy, perhaps the hapless reader is feeling weary with Chesterton. And irked with me.

"Grow up!" the protestors will cry. "Get on to something serious and sensational. Stop playing at life, the both of you. No human being, alive or dead, could be as happy as Chesterton pretended to be, including saints already bathed in the beatific vision. Do right by the man for once and focus on his battles, his sorrows, his losses, his drudgery, for we prefer to credit suffering as meritorious, not happiness. If you admire the man, as you claim, then stop insulting him by always putting his playful side forward, lest we think him a buffoon."

I pause to mount a defense.

Here it is. "Only meaningful work provides the soil in which festivity flourishes." These words come from the pen of Hugo Rahner in his study, *Man at Play*. In consecutive chapters Rahner considers the concept of play philosophically (man at play), theologically (God at play), ecclesiastically (the playing of the Church), and hopefully (the heavenly dance). He begins his renovation of the word *play* with Plato, who referred to man as a "*paigniontheo*"—a plaything of God. To suggest that creation is the result of the Creator's play may feel unsettling to some, but if it does, it is because they have shrunken God into their notion of play, instead of enlarging their notion of play to fit the lightness and freedom of God. Plato's pronouncement does not mean God acted in jest or in sport, it means that *play* is just the word we need to state the metaphysical truth that "the creation of the world and of humankind, although a divinely meaningful act, was by no means a necessary one." And that is how Rahner defines play: something meaningful but not necessary.

"Everywhere we find [in creation myths] an intuitive feeling that the world was not created under some kind of constraint; . . . rather it was born of a wise liberty, of the gay spontaneity of God's mind; in a word, it came from the hand of a child." Here is the significance of the medieval pictures of the infant Jesus carrying the sphere of the world in his hands, like a ball. If we lack a sense of play it is because we take ourselves too seriously. In order to have humor, one must have humility. I think we can all remember a time when we could not laugh at ourselves because our ego was wounded, and our playfulness was paralyzed, and we became very grave, indeed. Play is a daughter of modesty.

Play is a lightness and freedom of the spirit, and Chesterton thought "one characteristic of the great saints is their power of levity. Angels can fly because they can take themselves lightly. . . . The kings in their heavy gold and proud in their robes of purple will all of their nature sink downwards, for pride cannot rise to levity or levitation. Pride is the downward drag of all things into an easy solemnity. . . . For solemnity flows out of men naturally; but laughter is a leap. It is easy to be heavy; hard to be light. Satan fell by the force of gravity." Pride is ponderous.

Only meaningful work provides the soil in which festivity flourishes. Chesterton found his life's work meaningful in God's eyes, and was proportionably festive. Take the work away from Chesterton and you would not have festivity, you would have frivolity, which Rahner says is a sign of secret despair. He describes the frivolous person as someone "who cannot resist a joke; he will not keep his tongue off himself or anyone else, if he can raise a laugh, and will say things which a man of refinement would never say." Take the work away from Chesterton and you would not have Chesterton; you would have Oscar Wilde.

(Chesterton wrote: "Oscar Wilde said that sunsets were not valued because we could not pay for sunsets. But Oscar Wilde was wrong; we can pay for sunsets. We can pay for them by not being Oscar Wilde." Gratitude separates festivity from frivolity.)

The person who has taken the measure of the world by traversing its limits does not discover that he is nothing as compared to the world; he discovers that the world is nothing as compared to the Creator. That produces humility. This permits humor. And therefore Rahner says the inner essence of humor lies in the strength of the religious disposition: for what humor does is to note how far all earthly and human things fall short of the measure of God. Add to this the Christian conviction that God so loved the world that he entered it to play with us, and you will find the final key to festivity. "I am overwhelmed with an enormous sense of my own worthlessness—which is very nice and makes me dance and sing," Chesterton once wrote to Frances. And, he added, "neither with great technical charm."

RECOGNITION, THE HIGHER PLEASURE

From time to time we try to figure out how Chesterton got so much pleasure and joy out of the world. I am going to suggest a hypothesis. In doing so, I am apologetic and hesitant, because I rather dislike psychoanalyzing someone who cannot defend himself. But there may be some truth to the hypothesis, lightly treated.

Most of us think the greatest joy lies in new things. A new car (after our Neon came a Focus, and then a Honda and each one had better cup holders than the last); or a new device (after my laptop came an I touch, and now I have become expert on the Ipad); or a new wife (this one is purely hypothetical, and I have no examples to put in this parenthesis, thank God).

The new thing fascinates us because it is a new discovery, and we think discovering is the greatest joy. Columbus on the shores of the new world or Ferdinand cruising thru the straits of Magellan that now bear his name, Madam Curie corralling radiation or Einstein scribbling something about energy and matter with chalk dust in his hair. Newness, discovery, unearthing, unveiling, novelty, and originality impress us.

Now, here's my hypothesis. For Chesterton recognition was more enjoyable than discovery. And here's how I came to my hypothesis.

I was giving some lectures in Poland last spring, most graciously hosted by the Catholic University of Lublin (KUL), which had given us the use of an apartment for a few days. For the first few days, I admit that everything was delightful because it was new. But I was also discombobulated. Then all at once, walking across Lithuanian square, I suddenly recognized where I was— last night's restaurant is here, the shop where I bought my pen is there, the apartment is around the corner. If I had to, I could trace our way back to the street on which the McDonald's with the free WiFi was located.

And it occurred to me that while coming to something for the first time has its charm, coming to something for the second time has something more. It doesn't have to lose its charm, but it additionally embeds the discovered thing in an order. We were able to coordinate one thing with other things. Discovery only permits a gape-jawed stare; recognition permits us to make connections, both mental and geographical, because besides the thing, we see the order.

Chesterton's famous story of being more pleased by recognition than discovery is at the beginning of *Orthodoxy*. "I have often had a fancy for writing a romance about an English yachtsman who slightly miscalculated his course and discovered England under the impression that it was a new island in the South Seas." That Englishman gets turned around at sea in a storm, and lands again on the shore of England itself. "There will probably be a general impression that the man who landed (armed to the teeth and talking by signs) to plant the British flag on that barbaric temple which turned out to be the Pavilion at Brighton, felt rather a fool." But Chesterton doesn't mind a little tomfoolery. In fact, he envies the man. "His mistake was really a most enviable mistake; and he knew it, if he was the man I take him for. What could be more delightful than to have in the same few minutes all the fascinating terrors of going abroad combined with all the humane security of coming home again?"

The hero of *Orthodoxy* is someone who fails to discover, but comes to recognize. Chesterton says he set out to discover novel ideas, heretical ideas if that is what it took for them to be novel. And instead he landed on the shores of familiar territory. "For I am that man in a yacht. I discovered England. . . . The man from the yacht thought he was the first to find England; I thought I was the first to find Europe. I did try to found a heresy of my own; and when I had put the last touches to it, I discovered that it was orthodoxy." Only, he was not disappointed that the ideas were familiar, he recognized now how they coordinated.

A discovery can only be had once. Then its tail fades away like a dying comet. But recognition can be had again and again, and yet once more again, because Lithuanian Square can be come upon from every alleyway and avenue in Lublin. Recognition depends upon making a connection, and the thing we have discovered can now be recognized in connection with a hundred other things.

Chesterton recognizes that "If we saw the sun for the first time it would be the most fearful and beautiful of meteors." But that's the problem. We can only see it for the first time once. "Now that we see it for the hundredth time we call it, in the hideous and blasphemous phrase of Wordsworth, 'the light of common day.'" So then what is our recourse? We seek for the original thrill again, as Kierkegaard said of the aesthete, and we are forever restless. "We are inclined to demand six suns, to demand a blue sun, to demand a green sun." But Chesterton is content to recognize the sun come up again, and shine its light on an orderly world filled with things from Elfland. The fact that he can recognize, not merely discover, means there is no end to his delight.

PART 2
The Ordinary Home

"The chair I sit in is really romantic—nay, it is heroic, for it is eternally in danger."
July 31, 1909

AN INSIDE BIGGER THAN AN OUTSIDE

I have been having, for the last few days, a strange experience of space and time, only, it's not an experience of physics but an experience of psychology. My wife and I have been back in the town where we raised our family for thirteen years, the town where stands the house we lived in while the children were between the ages of three and sixteen. Of course, the first thing we did with our rented car was to drive to the old neighborhood, past that very sanctuary. Then we went down to the old grade school, which was a daily pilgrimage for little legs; and to the park where we would go sledding down a mountain which now looks like a molehill; and past Dave's Market known in its time for its penny candy, where young financiers could have their first experience of getting change for a nickel. And the phrase that keeps coming out of both our mouths is, "Look! It's so small." Neither of us can deny that this is the outstanding mark of our experience.

Why should that be?

There are a couple natural reasons why a space revisited would look small, but neither of those reasons apply. The first reason does not apply, that of a teenager returning to his elementary school and finding it smaller because he has become larger. He has to stoop to the water fountain, and can look straight into the top shelf of a locker he once had to reach on tiptoes. But neither Elizabeth nor I have grown any taller since leaving this fair city. The second reason does not apply, either, that of a person moving over the years from the apartment, to the starter home, to a suburban McMansion. I would predict that the square footage of our present house and this, our old house is almost the same footprint.

Yet it is still undeniable that the whole town feels like it has been washed in hot water and shrunk. What has happened?

C. S. Lewis uses a phrase several times in the *Chronicles of Narnia* that may explain the true cause. Tirian gets thrown into a stable to be killed by a monster, but finds himself standing in a great, green meadow before the High King Peter, and Queen Lucy. He looks through a crack in the door and sees the stable into which he had been tossed, and so concludes that the "Stable seen from within and the Stable seen from without are two different places." Peter confirms it by saying "Yes, Its inside is bigger than its outside." And Lucy reminds the reader that "In our world too, a stable once had something inside it that was bigger than our whole world." Again, at the end of Narnia itself, Lucy's sadness is soothed because she sees "This garden is like the Stable. It is far bigger inside than it was outside." "Of course, Daughter of Eve," said the Faun. "The further up and the further in you go, the bigger everything gets. The inside is larger than the outside."

I cannot say with any proof that Lewis took the thought from Chesterton, but I can say the thought is to be found in Chesterton. When Chesterton talks about the convert peering into the Catholic Church from the outside, he says the convert "often feels as if he were looking through a leper's window. He is looking through a little crack or crooked hole that seems to grow smaller as he stares at it; but it is an opening that looks towards the Altar. Only, when he has entered the Church, he finds that the Church is much larger inside than it is outside."

Chesterton was always interested in the capacious diminutive. In *Tremendous Trifles* he tells the story of Paul and Peter, two boys who lived chiefly in the front garden. When the fairy-milkman gave them their wishes, Paul wished "to be a giant that he might stride across continents and oceans and visit Niagara or the Himalayas in an afternoon dinner stroll." The milkman granted his wish, and Paul went on his way, only to find "Niagara it was no bigger than the tap turned on in the bathroom. He wandered round the world for several minutes trying to find something really large and finding everything small, till in sheer boredom he lay down on four or five prairies and fell asleep." Peter was smarter for making the opposite request, and asked to be made half an inch high. "When the transformation was over he found himself in the midst of an immense plain, covered with a tall green jungle and above which, at intervals, rose strange trees each with a head like the sun in symbolic pictures, with gigantic rays of silver and a huge heart of gold." (Chesterton loved dandelions.) This is the essay which contains his famous line, "The world will never starve for want of wonders; but only for want of wonder."

This is what was happening to us. The house seen from within, and the house seen from without are two different places. That puny-looking palace was once plenty large enough to put children to bed in, and feast nightly at table in, and conquer mathematics in, and annually dump Halloween candy onto the living floor in, and fit a Christmas tree into it, and hold all the love the world could ever know.

THIS OLD HOUSE

Any regular reader knows that I commonly benefit from the help of Mr. Gilbert Chesterton, but the reader would not know that I now need the help of Mr. Edward Chesterton unless I were to first remind the reader that Edward (who was Gilbert's father) was a house-agent, and, second, mention that we are now selling our house. The reason for our sale is the very happy occasion of new employment in a position that I dearly desired, but the last few weeks have involved the sad occasion of putting a house up for sale, and I have been thinking about houses and homes and Gilbert and Edward.

Gilbert described his father as someone who "sold houses for his living but filled his own house with his life." His father was not so foolish as to mistake his occupation for his life's identity, but instead, as so many Victorian Englishmen did, led "many parallel lives" in his hobbies, all of which he unfailingly put at the service of his children. He was to Gilbert and Cecil the "Man with the Golden Key" because he unlocked wonders for them. "His den or study was piled high with the stratified layers of about ten or twelve creative amusements; water-colour painting and modelling and photography and stained glass and fretwork and magic lanterns and mediaeval illumination. . . . He never dreamed of turning any of these plastic talents to any mercenary account, or of using them for anything but his own private pleasure and ours." I compunctiously admit that in the cleaning of our basement, I have not found any old water-color boxes of mine to discard, or wondered what to do with some leftover shard from a stained glass window I hadn't completed, or wondered what to do with any other half-used hobby resources. Instead, we have disposed of a broken radio, an uncompleted puzzle, and video games rendered obsolete by the latest, more powerful chip, and it is with a qualm that I admit my sloth in comparison with Edward's activity. Still, the central lesson Gilbert learned from his father was the very good lesson that "in everything that matters, the inside is much larger than the outside," which he found true of his house and I hope my children have found true of theirs.

There is no ordinary house, and there are no ordinary activities inside a house. All actions are pregnant with eternal consequence, which is why the pagans had the good sense to make a domestic religion, an idea not unfamiliar to most of Christianity. "So long as Christianity continued the tradition of patron saints and portable relics, this idea of a blessing on the household could continue. If men had not domestic divinities, at least they had divine domesticities. When Christianity was chilled with Puritanism and rationalism, this inner warmth or secret fire in the house faded on the hearth. But some of the embers still glow or at least glimmer; and there is still a memory among the poor that their material possessions are something sacred." I hope our house has been a sacred place.

The home is a place in which the average father or mother steps forward as expert by default, trying not to let their children know that they are performing *ad lib.* No special training is given to the master and mistress of a house, no expertise is required to rule one, which is just how Gilbert would have it. No specialists need apply. There are things that only experts can do, but there are things that we definitely want a person to do for himself, even if he does them badly. It is the essence of the democratic faith that "the most terribly important things must be left to ordinary men themselves—the mating of the sexes, the rearing of the young, the laws of the state." Or, in this case, the laws of the home, which is the ultimate democratic domain.

The phrase *ad lib* is short for *ad libitum,* which means "at the discretion of the performer," coming from *libere* which means "to please" (also the root of "love"). One can *ad lib* because in the home one can do what one pleases. Chesterton did. "The home is the only spot on earth where a man can alter arrangements suddenly, make an experiment or indulge in a whim. Everywhere else he goes he must accept the strict rules of the shop, inn, club, or museum that he happens to enter. He can eat his meals on the floor in his own house if he likes. I often do it myself; it gives a curious, childish, poetic, picnic feeling." The home is the stage for life's performance, and many things are done at the discretion of the performers. Even to the point of inviting unexpected cast members. In a letter to Frances while they were still engaged, Chesterton admits he would make no objection "to your having an occasional dragon to dinner, or a penitent Griffin to sleep in the spare bed" because home is where bad things are made good. Ours was a small house, but just large enough to exercise the dignity of those who dwelled within, just long enough to reach the human end of loving and being family, and just tall enough for us to stand up to iniquity. It has been a good house.

NOW WE'RE COOKING

My wife and I enjoy wandering through the Ikea store in Chicago from time to time, when we have the chance. Filled with Scandinavian designed products, the merchandise has a pleasing quality to the eye and an ingenious quality that fascinates my mind. I never thought a chair with that angle could be so comfortable and still hold my weight; I can't imagine why no one thought of such a simple corkscrew before; I am amazed at the versatility that results from putting a hinge here. It's like part museum and part inventor's workshop, and you can try out the exhibits.

Last visit we were walking through the kitchenware, and we stepped into a mock-up, sample kitchen layout, complete with stainless sinks and appliances, pine dish racks inside cupboards illuminated with track lighting, and a base-corner cabinet with more pull-out drawers than a Swiss army knife has blades. I exclaimed out loud, "Now, I could do some real cooking in a kitchen like this."

Apparently these words have escaped the lips of other Americans, too. Kitchen and Bath's Market Forecaster predicts that spending on kitchen renovations this year will reach nearly $80 billion. According to the Chicago Tribune, the average cost—and this is only an average—for remodeling a kitchen is $48,712. And one firm reached for comment recalls a job for $170,000. And yet, the Tribune observes an irony. "Even though Americans are cooking less, we're pumping more money than ever into souped-up kitchens" (I presume the pun was intentional).

Come to think of it, there was a time when I cooked more than I do now, and more than I might even if a contractor could shoehorn a $170,000 kitchen into our house. In the house where we raised our children my wife and I shared responsibilities in the kitchen pretty equally, but if there was any division of talent, hers was to make special meals more special, and mine was to make regular meals regularly. And I did not cook more then because we had a dual-fuel range with four star burners and electric griddle plus gas grill; I cooked more then because the four of us wanted to sit down to spaghetti and meatballs that evening. I did some real cooking in that kitchen, and it brought the realization that what inspires real cooking is not a combination microwave/convection oven/toaster oven, but a combination mother/father/child.

We cooked sweet and sour chicken in that kitchen while our boys were doing their math homework at the kitchen table, and their sums are still visible in the soft wood top. We mixed batter in that kitchen while gingerly stepping around the hot wheels track being laboriously set up around the table legs. We tried our hand at home-made egg rolls while toy dinosaurs roamed the floor, we rolled out cinnamon buns while He-Man and Skeletor were locked in mortal combat under foot, and we found we could play one hand of Uno between the time it took for each batch of cookies to come out of the oven.

So I have to wonder whether the cause of real cooking is the Wolfgang Puck celebrity endorsed Bistro collection on the top of the stove, or the family unit sitting round the table? And isn't that just like us, I can hear Chesterton chuckling. Our first instinct is to turn to our wallet and to a specialist. We would like to purchase what must be earned by discipline, we would have someone do for us what we must do for ourselves. We think the tool will train the hand. We put our hope in external things when the good we seek is an internal and eternal one. We suppose that progress in cookware technology can translate into progress in happiness. And if it's hard to afford both a $170,000 remodeling budget and a family of eight, we have an idea which we would shrink first to a less burdensome size. If we can't afford both, which will we choose?

Chesterton knew not of the kitchen craze, but the material and mechanical craze was already taking root. "My contempt boils over into bad behaviour when I hear the common suggestion that a birth is avoided because people want to be 'free' to go to the cinema or buy a gramophone or a loudspeaker." When people no longer feel that the child is more miraculous than the cinema, then something fundamental has been upended. The baby is

> a much more beautiful, wonderful, amusing and astonishing thing than any of the stale stories or jingling jazz tunes turned out by the machines. When men no longer feel that he is so, they have lost the appreciation of primary things, and therefore all sense of proportion about the world. People who prefer the

mechanical pleasures, to such a miracle, are jaded and enslaved. They are preferring the very dregs of life to the first fountains of life.

The kitchen hearth fire was a magical place for Chesterton, and can be for us, if we let the fire warm a human family, and not confine it in a box of stainless steel. Every normal man "wants an objective and visible kingdom; a fire at which he can cook what food he likes, a door he can open to what friends he chooses." In such a kitchen, one could do some real cooking.

HAM SANDWICH DISTRIBUTISM

Recently my wife and I had a dress rehearsal for the future. One son has been launched for a couple of years now and is living self-sufficiently, and last month our other son packed up his bass trombone for a three-week tour with his summer jazz band. This left Elizabeth and me staring into the future face of the empty nest syndrome, and it filled us with nostalgic memories. Summer family driving trips was one such memory that came vividly to mind, especially while she and I toured the back roads of Kentucky, Tennessee, and North Carolina. (I didn't say we sat home while we nursed our memories!)

Every trip is unique, but there may be some archetypical features to the family driving trip that you will recognize in both ours and yours. Father is always pushing to make a few more miles; the family groans when he announces that the first day's strike from Fargo to Billings will require a wake-up call at 4:30 a.m.; his idea of a good vacation is one so efficiently mapped out and smoothly executed that they could almost make it home two days early. Mother is the stable one in the car who is prepared to deal with any eventuality, from a flat tire to a grizzly bear, so long as it happens after morning coffee; she arbitrates disputes over who has more room in the back seat; she instinctively senses when one more ham and mustard sandwich will raise the level of mutinous intent beyond the breaking point and advises a restaurant lunch, despite what it will do to the budget, upon which she has had a firm grasp since the beginning. The children are oblivious in the back seat, passing time as children can before their minds develop a consciousness of time passing; they get about one hundred fifty miles to one Superman action figure and a bag of licorice; they live out of the present in expectation of the next moment.

Why do we do it? What drives us out of our comfortable home to lumpy mattresses and a diet of squashed sandwiches and warm cherry drink from a leaky thermos? Had you asked our family this question, we would have answered that we went "to see the west." Yet retrospect reveals a clearer answer, as memory usually does. There are 244,864 square miles in Wyoming and Montana combined, and Yellowstone Park itself is 3,472 square miles, but these days my memory serves up considerably smaller and more intense portions. For example, somewhere in Yellowstone, fifty feet up a trail I would never be able to find again, behind some bushes and through some trees, is a patch of ground not much larger than our front yard that has sagebrush and a rapid stream that can float grass and sticks and a Superman action figure tied to a string, and there is a rock with the best place for resting a plastic cup of warm cherry drink while you eat a ham and mustard sandwich. If God granted me a great, miraculous weighing device, and I could put those 244,864 square miles on one tray and that little patch of ground on the other, I know which would be the weightier.

The Jewish theologian Abraham Heschel wrote, "We must not forget that it is not a thing that lends significance to a moment; it is the moment that lends significance to things." I could adapt his words, and say it is not the size of the acreage that lends significance to the place; it is the preciousness of the picnic which lends significance to the west.

I think this discovery is something of a key to Chesterton's notion of Distributism. It seems to me that Chesterton did not propose his "creed of small proprietorship" because he supposes there is something inherently better in smallness, or because he thinks small shops a more efficient means of production than large factories, or because he is a Marxist, or because he is a Capitalist. He proposed Distributism because he thinks it is not the size of the factory that lends significance to the work; it is the dignity of the worker that lends significance to the labor. The soul is weightier than the tonnage on the bill of lading, like the picnic was made up of something more eternal than the mountains in which it took place. The human dignity of the proprietor, even the proprietor of a small shop or a small farm, is weightier, on balance, than 244,864 widgets crated and shipped to market. The Distributist proprietor does not exist merely to produce for others, or to consume what others produce, and we damage workers' dignity when we think they only work to feed the appetite of the state; they have mouths of their own to feed before the nest empties. The workers should have the leisured satisfaction of preparing and consuming their own ham and mustard sandwiches.

The modern world has it wrong when it says leisure exists for the sake of work. We do not take vacations to get rested up in order to work harder. Rather, work exists for the sake of leisure, and Distributism blends labor with the leisured home in a way modern systems do not. If I was today asked "what is the west for?" I would answer, with the privilege memory affords, "for having picnics in."

THE ORDINARILY MIRACULOUS

I suppose it's only harmless vanity that makes us want to increase the significance of our work in the eyes of others. To want to exalt our occupational station must be rooted in human nature ever since Adam and Eve ate the fruit and put on their vita "ex-gardeners." It's hard on the ego to describe oneself by the old vocabulary (garbage man) when new rhetoric is available (sanitation engineer). But pity the circumstances of the poor academic! How could he or she compete in a television special about the world's most mysterious professions? This culture does not exactly fibrillate over the description "reads books for a living." One might try to earn some bonus credits for writing one, but even that accomplishment can be relativized by a swift comment. The Christmas after my first book appeared, one of my two boys was teasing the other about how much better his presents were going to be by belittling what the other could expect. "You're just getting underwear," he said provokingly, to which the other replied, "Oh yeah? Well, you're getting Papa's book." Apparently there is something lower than what I thought was the lowest rung on the Christmas present chain.

Using a foreign language will often add mystery to a state of affairs which otherwise sounds quite dull, and French is especially good for this, so I thought about telling people that I do *séances* for a living. The word simply means "a sitting" or "session," deriving from *seoir* which means "to sit," and it is, in fact, the position I assume to complete my daily chores. But, of course, in ordinary English this French word has picked up the additional meaning of being a meeting of minds with dead people, and were such a suspicion to attach itself to my daily routine it could only help my reputation. And given the authors I usually read, it's technically true, too.

Of course, I know that when investigative reporting reveals my fraud, the meeting I have with Aristotle or Augustine will seem less spectacular than what takes place in a curtained room with a crystal ball. But does the fact it is less spectacular mean it should be less astonishing? Chesterton took pains to teach us to pause before we give our answer to this query. He wanted to teach us to remember the wondrous quality of ordinary things even if they no longer appear sensational to us. He said that

> Just as we all like love tales because there is an instinct of sex, we all like astonishing tales because they touch the nerve of the ancient instinct of astonishment. This is proved by the fact that when we are very young children we do not need fairy tales: we only need tales. Mere life is interesting enough. . . . These tales say that apples were golden only to refresh the forgotten moment when we found that they were green. They make rivers run with wine only to make us remember, for one wild moment, that they run with water.

There is a story about a community that prayed for a miracle to prove the divine, and the deity responded by making the river stop flowing on the Sabbath. The people were amazed, and every Sabbath they brought their children to the riverbank to show them the unnatural pause, and they brought their children, and they brought their children, until the day someone said, "So what? The river always stops on the Sabbath." On that day the miracle ceased, not because it stopped happening but because it ceased to be miraculous. Say to someone, "Look! The sun rose today," and you're likely to receive the same response given at the riverside: it always happens like this. So Chesterton pricks us by suggesting that perhaps "God says every morning, 'Do it again' to the sun; and every evening, 'Do it again' to the moon. It may not be automatic necessity that makes all daisies alike; it may be that God makes every daisy separately, but has never got tired of making them."

In my case, then, I should realize that my academic *séance* is actually the more miraculous, because it stands upon a thousand miracles, whereas a superstitious *séance* would stand upon only one. Were it possible that a dead spirit might communicate with the living, it would require no more than a momentary breach in the veil. But in order for my mind, and the minds of my students, to meet the great thinkers of the past in the ordinary way, a myriad of miracles are required. It depends upon the development of language, speech, and alphabet; the invention of parchment and pen, and the employment of scribes; it has required the printing of books, the shelving of books by turn in monastery and university, the marketing of books, and the development of a whole culture that valued books enough to commit to this arduous task— why, practically the whole of human history had to throw its shoulder into the accomplishment of civilization just to make it possible for us to meet the minds of Plato and Gregory. The book in my hand is as magical as a golden apple, or a goblet scooped from a river of wine, if I see it as Chesterton would. There is nothing ordinary in being.

ONE WORLD AT A TIME

The other night we found ourselves in the difficulty of wishing to wile away the evening with some relaxed viewing but found nothing whatsoever of merit on television. This is not particularly unusual, but what we thought to do about it was unusual, at least we haven't done it for a while. We pulled out old movies of family vacations. I am not as rabid a cinematographer as some fathers you might read about, or meet, or might be, but I have threaded my share of magnetic tape through the recording heads. Thus we had ample selection to suit our cozy and nostalgic mood among such hits as "Yellowstone 1988" or "Grand Canyon 1990" or "California 1995."

After watching for an hour I faced a realization and a lesson. The realization came from the lesson. The realization was that I am not as good as a cinematographer as I thought, though this was not due to any deficiency of an aesthetic-technical kind. I had well-composed frames of Old Faithful against a blue sky, scenic explorations of color on canyon walls as my zoom lens crawled up them like a spider, and a slow crawl along the panoramic vista of the Pacific Ocean. The lesson I learned was that what interested me when I took the pictures does not interest me now.

We have shots of a buffalo in a meadow, of flowers in a garden at San Jose, of sea otters bobbing in the surf, and, at the time, I took the pictures with the confidence that family and coerced friends would want to view these rare and uncommon sights over and over. But the other night, all that interested me was seeing pictures of my children. I was distressed to see their heads enter into frame right, only to exit frame left so I could scan up a sequoia tree. I couldn't hear my kids' voices over the noise of the surf I was wading in to film some floating kelp. And just as I began to recognize the familiar gait that once belonged to the busy legs of an eight-year-old, they disappeared from the screen in preference for a long, slow surveillance of the rocks on which they were climbing. Although that sequoia has seen a century come and go, and the surf has pounded that sand since the dinosaurs, and millennia will have to pass before that granite peak will erode, I now wish I had captured images of something longer-lasting, more ageless, more eternal than they.

Chesterton saw eternity in every child, a union of the universal with the particular, a gift from the heavens cached with unsuspecting mortals. He could not imagine the reasoning behind the developing social suggestion that a birth be avoided "because people want to be 'free' to go to the cinema or buy a gramophone." They have overlooked where freedom exists. "Now a child is the very sign and sacrament of personal freedom. He is a fresh free will added to the wills of the world. . . . He is also a much more beautiful, wonderful, amusing and astonishing thing than any of the stale stories or jingling jazz tunes turned out by the machines. When men no longer feel that he is so, they have lost the appreciation of primary things, and therefore all sense of proportion about the world."

Chesterton would have made a wonderful father, and it was a blow to both he and Frances that she was unable to bear children. Instead, the two of them created a home in Beaconsfield designed to be "a nest even if there were to be no nestlings," where youngsters were positively welcomed. Adults were excluded from the Christmas parties, and, in the absence of nurses or parents, the children would hang on Gilbert's neck in affection. He and Frances devised endless games, and constructed a toy theatre such as his father had made for him. There is the story of a small guest at such a party "who was asked when he got home whether Mr. Chesterton had been very clever. 'I don't know about clever,' was the reply, 'but you should see him catch buns in his mouf.'" Dorothy Collins, his secretary, remembers that her three-year-old daughter was shy around adults, and to win her over, and lure her over to him, Gilbert casually took out the seven inch long knife he always carried and began to open and shut the blade, not looking in her direction. "Next she was on his knee. A little later we heard her remark, 'Uncle Gilbert, you make jokes just like my Daddy.' And from him came, 'I do my best.'"

But let Chesterton speak for himself.

> Grass and children
> There seems no end to them.
> But if there were but one blade of grass

Men would see that it is fairer than lilies,
And if we saw the first child
We should worship it as the God come on earth.

Unlike some cinematographers who feel duty bound to store up as much scenery as possible for later review, he took a narrower vision. He saw one child at a time, one blade of grass at a time, one world at a time, because though there seem to be no end to the days of childhood, there actually is. He saw eternity, and my wide-angle lens drank in plenty of scenery, but nothing sacramental.

THE SONG OF NOTTING HILL

One early, bright morning as I was crossing campus, the chirping of a bird could not be ignored for standing out so vividly against the stillness of the morning. With a little searching I was able to spot him. He was on the top twig of the highest branch of the tallest tree at the center of the courtyard, chattering proudly. It was a near perfect Disney moment, and at any moment I expected to see Thumper appear from under the hedge and the bird descend lightly to Bambi's antlers. Then I recalled something I had read somewhere. It is an ornithological theory that when birds sing like that they are laying claim to their territory. They do with their song what dogs do with their urine: they mark boundaries. Birds sing to establish and maintain territories, and therefore this may be interpreted as aggressive behavior. Instead of singing rapturously, the bird was singing offensively. And that little sparrow was as pleased with himself as Alexander the Great, Genghis Khan, or Napoleon. His territory! His domain! The instinct lies deep in the creature.

The instinct lies deep in the human creature too. Chesterton was a romantic, but he did not ignore facts, and it is a fact that human beings share the proclivity of all creatures to carve out domains by performing idealistic and heroic acts, what some might term aggressive behavior. This is the premise of Adam Wayne, the Napoleon of Notting Hill, creator of a nation by the same name in Chesterton's novel. Notting Hill was a rather tedious place until dressed up with banners and borders, after which it became a place for patriotism. Chesterton valued small republics. When asked once on tour how big a republic should be, he replied that the hotel in which he was staying would be just fine. For it is not the size of the empire that makes us admire an emperor. If I were now, instantaneously, declared king of lifeless Jupiter I should deserve less respect than if I ruled ten acres of land in such a way that it produced a fine harvest of turnips. What we admire is courage, creativity, resourcefulness, responsibility, and not size alone. A home is large enough to be a kingdom with the imperial pleasure of making laws about bedtime, and tending one's own hearth fire, and granting boons in the serious matter of eating supper on the living room floor as an indoor picnic.

I speculate, then, that our natural desire for a kingdom might not be an evil, since I share it with brer fox and brer bird. The creatures do not sin, so my natural inclination to rule might not be wicked. The Christian tale says man and woman were told to take dominion over wild and anarchic processes in the name of a king on a far distant shore. Planting flags, and growing civilizations, and chirping songs of victory with our feathers ruffled and a lump of pride in our throats may be a stepping-stone to the Kingdom of God, for when I become king over my dominion, then I will have a dominion to hand over to my King. Humility is not some sham pretending that I am not a king when I am in fact lord over the field and the beasts in it and the bird in that tree. My sin is less the desire to make a kingdom, than the unwillingness to submit that kingdom to the true King when I'm done.

Charles Williams wrote that there are two ways to this King: the way of negation and the way of affirmation. The former looks the more impressive because it is the more dramatic, with its monastic vows of poverty, chastity and obedience, but the way of affirmation is no less a way to God. Catholicism has taught that even as the monk flees the world in order to journey to God, he or she must confess that it is also possible to reach the same transcendent God through the world. The same Church that acclaimed celibacy recognized marriage as a sacrament. Williams says the first poet of the way of affirmation was Dante. And Dante is presented with two keys at the end of his journey. Williams writes, "The keys are also the methods of Rejection and Affirmation. Rejection is a silver key, which is 'more dear'; Affirmation is a golden key, more difficult to use. Yet both are necessary for any life."

I would submit that Chesterton is an equal to Dante in this matter. He knows that "any human tradition would make more of the heroes who suffered for something than of the human beings who simply benefited by it, but that does not alter the fact that there are more human beings than heroes." Chesterton also admired ordinary human beings as they used their golden key to unlock a doorway to the sublime in the everyday. By ruling their homes they are servant in the Reign of God; by loving their spouses they get a foretaste of heaven; by struggling to attain the natural virtues of prudence and courage they are capacitated to receive the supernatural virtues of faith, hope and love; by sacrificing a temporal good they develop the spiritual muscle to sacrifice for an eternal good.

All this that bird told me in his Napoleonic song.

BONDS OR BUBBLES?

The attentive reader might have noticed a pattern to this column over the months. I usually try to lure the reader into a Chesterton passage by means of describing an encounter with something in the world that reminded me of it. However, being ever in pursuit of novelty, creativity, and originality, I shall not follow this pattern today. In fact, I shall reverse it. I shall write my column backwards.

I begin, then, by concluding with my recollection of this Chestertonian moment: "If we all floated in the air like bubbles, free to drift anywhere at any instant, the practical result would be that no one would have the courage to begin a conversation. It would be so embarrassing to start a sentence in a friendly whisper, and then have to shout the last half of it because the other party was floating away into the free and formless ether." I can still remember smiling at the thought of comparing two people to two soap bubbles, drifting away from each other on a summer breeze, shouting and signaling as they recede from mutual sight. Who else would compare people to such unstable things as bubbles or dandelion fluff on the air currents?

Taking one step backward, I proceed. The context for this Chesterton bon mot is a discussion of marriage. He asserts that "in everything worth having, even in every pleasure, there is a point of pain or tedium that must be survived, so that the pleasure may revive and endure." "The success of the marriage comes after the failure of the honeymoon." Sometimes a point of honor is required as the cause of a commitment that goes beyond the mood and finds the resolution. "It is amply sufficient to justify the general human feeling of marriage as a fixed thing, dissolution of which is a fault, or at least, an ignominy." (C. S. Lewis similarly remarked that divorce should surely be seen more like cutting off an arm than like dissolving a cartel.)

But this makes Chesterton sound like an old grump! "In everything on this earth that is worth doing, there is a stage when no one would do it, except for necessity or honor. It is then that the Institution upholds a man and helps him on to the firmer ground ahead." Take your medicine, even if it's bitter. I never promised you a rose garden. Stiff upper lip. Puritanical self-denial. And this does not sound like the Chesterton I've met on a hundred other pages. He is an incurable romantic and idealist. He takes a trip through fairy land on every hansom cab ride to the office; his home is a castle where he and Queen Francis rule in playful anarchy; so why does he say such things?

The key is given in the next line: "The essential element is not so much duration as security." Once again, for Chesterton the structure exists to preserve life, not stifle it. As grammar imposes order upon a sentence so that we can speak, marriage imposes security upon a relationship so that love flourish. "Two people must be tied together in order to do themselves justice; for twenty minutes at a dance, or for twenty years in a marriage." And then follows the quote with which I began: if husband and wife were soap bubbles who drifted on the winds of change, without control or choice, then the practical result would be that they would fear to begin a conversation. "The two must hold each other to do justice to each other."

In conclusion, I now come to the beginning of my column.

Elizabeth and I had a fight the other day. That in itself is not so remarkable (although I hope the gentle reader thinks well enough of me to think it at least somewhat remarkable, and not frequent). Our arguments have become smaller and rarer after living in sacrament for thirty-one years, and usually one person or the other is in enough self-control to head off the misunderstanding at the pass. But sometimes we push each other's buttons simultaneously, and then we are each so riled that no one wants to go to the pass to head off anything. In Japanese swordsmanship there is a term translated as "mutual kill" used to describe an occurrence where the attacker and defender strike so simultaneously that they both die; our more heated arguments happen when there has been a "mutual zinger."

Normally resolution comes with the passage of time, which cools the blood and restores equilibrium. I think men especially prefer this strategy. When men want to make up, they tend not to return to the uncomfortable moment and confront it (something someone who was not an emotional coward could do), instead they drop little hints, make small jokes, are obviously helpful around the kitchen, and watch for an approaching light in the darkness. But the day after this particular argument, Elizabeth and I were scheduled to drive twelve hours in the car over the course of two days. Faced with close quarter confinement inside a box of steel, we took the morning to speed up the reconciliation process. Marriage bonds are useful for bringing people face to face like that. After all, if we floated in the air like bubbles, free to drift anywhere, no one would have the courage to begin a conversation.

THE FREEDOM TO RESTORE

One of the comments one is apt to hear around the time of Christmas, or shortly after, is that "it was nice while it lasted." I suppose it is possible that the comment is casually dropped simply as an observation about the temporal nature of all things, but I don't think so. I think the comment is usually made in some other spirit. It could be meant regretfully, uttered with a sad sigh that the sparkle of the season has waned, and food has become ordinary again, and our reasons for fellowship have ended. It could be meant parentally, uttered with a raised eyebrow intended to remind us that we're grown-ups, after all, and too much pleasantness will make us forget our real task, which is to do our duty and make something of ourselves and find important things to accomplish now that this recess is over. It can even be meant Scroogishly, uttered in an attempt to spoil the fun of people who are enjoying something that a deep, incapacitating fear prevents Scrooge from enjoying. (Medieval philosophers called this vice "envy," which meant being saddened by another's good fortune, and gladdened by another's misfortune.)

Whatever the motivation, I can almost already hear people sighing, censuring, or snickering that the calm, the twilight, the luminescence, the jubilation, the love of Christmas cannot last. And I can almost hear Chesterton asking, Why not?

One of the fundamental expressions of the human freedom with which Chesterton credited the ordinary man and woman was their ability to choose how they wanted to live. When told that we must docilely accept whatever the future holds, that we are not free to rebuild our homes according to the blueprint of a happier time, Chesterton replied, Why not? "This is the first freedom that I claim: the freedom to restore. I claim a right to propose as a solution the old patriarchal system of a Highland clan, if that should seem to eliminate the largest number of evils. . . . I claim the right to propose the complete independence of the small Greek or Italian towns, a sovereign city of Brixton or Brompton, if that seems the best way out of our troubles. . . . I merely claim my choice of all the tools in the universe; and I shall not admit that any of them are blunted merely because they have been used." The Christmas pictures make it seem that the society that had time for family is old-fashioned and has gone the way of the horse and buggy, but even without the horse and without the buggy, aren't we free to restore what was good in that society?

Flabbergasted, the pragmatic analyst might sputter that we cannot turn back the clock to simpler times, to which Chesterton might politely point out that we can. Indeed, we have during the Christmas season. "There is one metaphor of which the moderns are very fond; they are always saying, 'You can't put the clock back.' The simple and obvious answer is 'You can.' A clock, being a piece of human construction, can be restored by the human finger to any figure or hour. In the same way society, being a piece of human construction, can be reconstructed upon any plan that has ever existed." This season is pooh-poohed as nostalgic, but *nostos* means to return home, and if we find the social relationships we experience at Christmas preferable to the society we keep the rest of the year, which is our real home?

Reeling, Chesterton's high-minded dialogue partner would struggle to imagine what it would be like if we kept up such a home. Chesterton would help develop his friend's withered faculty of imagination by recalling the whimsy permitted in the free home. Here is "the only spot on earth where a man can alter arrangements suddenly, make an experiment or indulge in a whim. Everywhere else he goes he must accept the strict rules of the shop, inn, club, or museum that he happens to enter. He can eat his meals on the floor in his own house if he likes. I often do it myself; it gives a curious, childish, poetic, picnic feeling." We have been childishly poetic all Christmas long, smiling and singing and decorating trees in the living room; why stop now, to become prosaic and dull?

So, then, why can't Christmas last? Why not extend the freedoms we have felt to the whole year? Why should we obey the dictatorial tyranny of clock or calendar? Why should compassion be only seasonal? Why let the preferential option for the poor expire? Why can't a small society, composed of whoever desires it badly enough, maintain the freedom to give, instead of acquire? Why not continue to choose the greater spiritual good over inferior material goods? Why not continue to make time for feasting with friends and baking cookies with children? Why can't the love that danced between the Holy Family in the crèche be reproduced in every holy family, in whatever city they inhabit? If we have found the garden in which we have been playing to be more gratifying than the desert from which we came, why go back? If we have preferred our behavior of late, why stop? If, as Chesterton says, there is nothing quite like the warmth of Christmas, why don't we remain cloaked in it? Why not?

BC AND AD

Few things seem as permanent as the biological bond between parent and child. Elizabeth and I find ourselves reflecting on this fact as our last fledgling has this year grown his flight feathers and flown the coop to roost in a college dorm. The nest is empty now, but we don't feel any less parental toward either of our two boys for it. It started me thinking about how binding is the blood bond. Even in a new house, old memories linger—of Lego blocks and homework at the table and clean feet pajamas.

Modern folk who are impressed with biology like to talk about an evolution of nature that naturally makes us protective parental units. These folk like to talk about millions of years of evolution developing a parental instinct that we share with certain species of animals (though not those species that eat their young). But then I look around the house and I notice something more permanent than this biological bond. I notice the marital bond. The children are gone, but Elizabeth and I are still here!

Spirit trumps nature. The supernatural bond is more permanent than the natural one. The biological bond is deep, but the spiritual bond is lofty, and it carries us to unexpected heights. We are marveling that as once we were husband and wife BC (before children), we still are husband and wife AD (after departure). For a number of years we thought being two was normal and we couldn't imagine anything else; then we were doubled to make four and for two decades plus that felt normal; now that we are two again, we are not halved but feel fuller than we ever did. Being two AD seems more than, not just equal to, being two BC, even though the head count at night is the same. But, then, marriage always was a matter of strange arithmetic. It has been said that marriage does not involve just two people but three (meaning God), but when counting persons on my Trinitarian fingers I get five.

"Man is a quadruped," Chesterton said; a strange arithmetic, indeed. This is the sole text for today's meditation. A man and a woman is not one plus one to make two—that would be a business alliance. Neither are they one plus one to make one—that would be a business merger. Nor are they a half plus a half, like a centaur, with the top half ruling the bottom half. The supernatural relationship of which I stammer to speak cannot be founded on the weakness of one or the neediness of the other; it must come from a superabundance.

Elizabeth and I are like Adam and Eve walking around in the Garden of Eden, even if my love handles are a little more developed than a renaissance artist might depict Adam's to be in his state of paradise. I feel as blessed to see Elizabeth appear around the corner the millionth time as Adam felt when Eve made her appearance the first time. We even have an advantage on them. They were just newlyweds, tentatively getting to know one another, while we have three decades of memories feeding into our relationship. And all the memories are good, although I need Dante to explain how that can be.

Dante says that at the summit of Mount Purgatory is the Earthly Paradise, the place of man's innocence. It is from here that, if man had not fallen, he would have entered upon the life of Perfection, in this world and the next. Dorothy Sayers describes that passage into paradise this way.

> God wastes nothing—not even sin. The soul that has struggled and come through is enriched by its experiences, and Grace does not merely blot out the evil past but in the most literal sense "makes it good." The sin is not forgotten, either by God or by the soul: it is forgiven, and so made the occasion of a new and still more blessed relationship; Redeemed Man is a creature made more precious to his Creator than unfallen man could have been. Accordingly, in Dante's Earthly Paradise [the Forest at the very top of Mt. Purgatory], the soul has to drink of the twin streams of Lethe and Eunoe. The first destroys all memory of evil and sin with it; the second restores remembrance of the sin, but only as an historical fact and as the occasion of grace and blessedness.

Nothing in our marriage has been wasted. All the memories, even memories of sins, are now good memories because they have drunk from the twin streams and been transfigured. This is a gift husbands and wives give each other. But it is a hard spiritual work, one that fifty percent of marriages today seem unwilling to do.

"Paradise" comes from an old Iranian dialect which combined "pairi" (around) and "daeza" (wall). It meant a walled garden or orchard, such as the one that the author of Genesis 2 said God planted. The Israelites carried a portable temple through the wilderness, one they could roll up in the evening and take with them; we carry a portable paradise that we take with us wherever we go. Wherever the four walls of the domestic castle are raised up, it is the orchard of Eden.

PART 3
Social Reform

*"In practical politics the survival of the fittest
frequently means only the survival of the fussiest."*
August 8, 1925

NUDGE AND JUDGE

I was recently asked to compose an editorial for a journal to which I subscribe. The invitation carried the stipulation that the editorial be "opinionated," as in "editorials should be topical and opinionated," but before that publication receives its editorial, I am distracted to write something about the process of writing editorials. I hope the other journal gets its piece eventually.

I'm sure the request for an opinionated editorial sounds reasonable to the average person, but the average person is not hampered, as I am, by a Scandinavian character. We are a mild-mannered and mediatorial people, and in order to become opinionated I thought I had to become pugnacious. I resolved to be truculent on all subjects, at all times. So it happened during my calisthenics that a stray remark provoked an argument within my head as to whether large is better than small. First I contentiously rose to the defense of small, pointing out that it is tidy, trim, precious, manageable, delicate, refined, and unpretentious. Then I disputatiously pointed out that large is expansive, magnanimous, plenteous, sturdy, commanding, substantial, and capacious.

Alas, at the end of the drill I was stopped short by an observation, the observation that sidetracked me to this reflection. I realized that my whole argument was all adjective, and no noun. There were so many vivid associations with each word that in the heat of opinionated dispute it felt like a real argument, but anyone eavesdropping on my practice session would do me in by asking, "Is a large *what* better than a small *what*?" At which point it struck me that most of our political quarrels or religious feuds are mostly adjectival recoils. Someone incautiously asserts that liberalism is better for being open, lenient, clement, philanthropic, beneficent, reformative, and prodigal, to which someone contentiously rises to the defense of conservatism as ancient, enduring, inveterate, discreet, circumspect, prudent and traditional. (The helpfulness of a thesaurus in adjectival arguing should not go unnoticed.) We need someone—maybe Chesterton—to whisper into our barren debates, "But *what* do you want to conserve? *What* do you want to liberate?"

Few people are as opinionated as Chesterton, but I would not call him quarrelsome, since he professed that "the principal objection to a quarrel is that it interrupts an argument," and since his opinion results not from adjectives, but from thought about a thing. Surely eternal values like human dignity, and the family, and the mystery of the Mass want conserving; but surely the poor want liberation from unjust systems, and women from prejudices that stifle their full dignity, and worshipers from perfunctorily performing priests.

I think, then, that I've hit upon why our arguments are so unfruitful, but my explanation would benefit from personifying the two parties involved. When Chesterton wanted to personalize progressives and conservatives he called them Hudge and Gudge. Since he has already taken the letters "H" and "G," I will pick two other letters from the alphabet, completely at random, with no particular significance, and call them Nudge and Judge.

Nudge desires to rectify the world's faults; he is filled with the restless, creative, God-given energy to imagine new possibilities and, after envisioning them, bring them to realization; he incites and provokes, agitates and instigates. Judge, by contrast, desires to conserve a hard-won heritage; he is filled with the grounded, providential, God-given energy to preserve accomplished goods; he sustains life by tending its boundaries, and preserves liberty by protecting from chaos. But the reason why today's Nudge and Judge find it difficult to hold a civil conversation is because they lack a common subject. The subject of Nudge's attention is the world, while the subject of Judge's attention is Nudge.

Chesterton nudged. He did so when he supported distributism and Ireland's independence; he did so as comrades-in-arms with his brother Cecil and Belloc on the *New Witness*; he opposed the popular Boer war with an unpopular attack on jingoism; and he befriended the right a besieged lower class had to home and self-rule and beer.

And Chesterton judged. He wrote,

> In the matter of reforming things, as distinct from deforming them, there is one plain and simple principle; a principle which will probably be called a paradox. There exists in such a case a certain institution of law; let us say, for the sake of simplicity, a fence or gate erected across a road. The more modern type

of reformer goes gaily up to it and says, "I don't see the use of this; let us clear it away." To which the more intelligent type of reformer will do well to answer: "If you don't see the use of it, I certainly won't let you clear it way. Go away and think. Then, when you can come back and tell me that you *do* see the use of it, I may allow you to destroy it."

Judge's flaw is to be so distracted by his self-appointed task of being his brother Nudge's keeper that he neglects to put his own shoulder to the wheel; Nudge's flaw is to see from his narrow perspective, without due regard for ancient and wider vision. Judge's sin is condescension, Nudge's sin is conceit. But in fact, Judge needs Nudge's energy, and Nudge needs Judge's perspective, and Chesterton had both, and I will be disappointed if I let one prevail over the other in myself.

GO AHEAD, ASK ME!

When Chesterton was courting his fiancée, Frances, he wrote a letter to her containing the same cockeyed view of things exhibited in his other writings. He listed the assets he could offer her, and mentioned a Straw Hat, a Walking Stick, a copy of Whitman's poems, and a pocket knife. Not just an ordinary pocket knife, he said, but one that contained an element for taking stones out of a horse's hoof. "What a beautiful sensation of security it gives one," he wrote, "to reflect that if one should ever have enough money to buy a horse and should happen to buy one and the horse should happen to have a stone in his hoof—that one is ready; one stands prepared, with a defiant smile!"

I come before you today, gentle reader, with that same defiant smile, a smile arising from the beautiful sensation of being securely prepared for a contingency. Should a person one day engage me in conversation about Chesterton, and should it happen that this person make a personal inquiry of me, and should the inquiry happen to be what is my favorite quote from the Chestertonian corpus, I am ready; I stand prepared, with a defiant smile! I have identified the passage that encapsulates Chesterton for me, which explains the sway he holds over me, which summarizes what it is about his philosophy that can free the modern mind. In light of how quotable Chesterton is, you can imagine what a relief it was to come to this determination; the sheer number of claimants to the distinction of being "my favorite quote" is enough to cause sleepless nights.

From my being a Catholic, you might think the quote comes from one of Chesterton's apologetical works on the Church, but it does not. From my being an academic, you might think the quote comes from one of his historical biographies, but it does not. From my being a bit of an nonconformist, you might think it comes from one of his essays on distributism, but it does not. It comes from Chesterton's delicious book entitled *Heretics*, in a chapter called "On the Negative Spirit," in a paragraph where he defends Victorian society, about which I know next to nothing.

Chesterton's contemporaries, being very modern, faulted the Victorians for not being very modern, for being antiquated, for being out-of-fashion and behind the times. Their fault, everyone said, was that they lacked a realistic view of the world. Like ostriches with their heads in the sand, they would not face up to the sterner realities afflicting the modern man and modern woman. To Chesterton's contemporaries, the Victorians looked bewildered, clumsy, and perplexed—like startled deer caught in the harsh headlights of a brave new world where morals and mores and manners had changed too quickly for them to keep up. In short, the Victorians were accused of being prudish.

This way of thinking draws battle lines between the modernist and the prude. The left and the right, the liberal and the conservative, the revolutionary and the reactionary stoop down at this point to pick up stones to throw at each other's glass houses. The one party knows the times they are a'changing, and the other party appears hopelessly out of touch because their ears still burn during sex scenes in the movies, they are cowed by profanity, they refuse to consider Rap a kind of music, and they complain about declining standards on television.

Now, if my only choice was realist or irrelativist, it is only too easy for me to choose to walk forward with the liberal instead of backward with the conservative. Were I asked, I would identify myself as liberal. Who wants to be considered a prude? One must live in the real world, after all.

But this is exactly where my favorite quote of Chesterton applies, for he gives me another option choice. He cuts across this glib division with a wave of his analytical wand, and creates one more choice than the two offered me. His philosophy (or point of view, if you like) creates more freedom for me than I had before. He says that what disgusted the Victorian, and very justly so, "was not the presence of a clear realism, but the absence of a clear idealism." That's the quote. Chesterton suggests there is a third alternative between being right for the wrong reason and being wrong for the right reason. One should be right for the right reason. Beside the alternative of accepting anything or rejecting everything, there is a third option of embracing what contributes to a realistic good and remaining critical of what falls short of an ideal good.

It is possible, then, that when one does not swallow everything the future dishes up, it is not because one fears the real world, but rather because one is examining it in the light of an ideal. One's objection to coarse language and crude behavior and ill-mannered incivility and uncovenanted sex would not be because one opposes change, but because one opposes change that degrades the human being. And if one believes there are ideals to be obeyed, then one becomes a creature even more rare in captivity than a thoughtful conservative; one becomes an obedient liberal. "Strong and genuine religious sentiment has never had any objection to realism; on the contrary, religion was the realistic thing, the brutal thing, the thing that called names."

SEE YOU IN THE FUNNY PAPERS

People one generation older than me use the phrase "See you in the funny papers." Never entirely sure what it meant, I assumed it was saying someone was comical enough to fit as a character in Li'l Abner, Andy Capp, or Pogo.

I came across an article in the online version of *The Daily Mail* that I thought was comical, though it wasn't supposed to be a funny paper. The headline read, "Holland proposes giving over-70s the right to die if they 'consider their lives complete.'" The paper did not intend for either the subject or their reporting to be funny, but nearly every sentence caused a yokel's grin on my face. I offer this recap of my interior dialogue, with the newspaper's lines italicized.

"Assisted suicide for anyone over 70 who has simply had enough of life is being considered in Holland." I can imagine having had enough of supper, enough of television, even enough of this newspaper, but how can one have had enough of life? This seems to suppose that we are containers to be filled to a brim line, instead of poets and lovers who can reflect the infinite.

"Non-doctors would be trained to administer a lethal potion to elderly people who 'consider their lives complete.'" This is a convenient way around that pesky Hippocratic oath.

"The radical move would be a world first and push the boundaries even further in the country that first legalized euthanasia." It must be good if boundaries are being pushed. We are advancing beyond the narrow-mindedness of our ancestors who harbored some irrational prejudice in favor of staying alive.

"The Dutch parliament is to debate the measure after campaigners for assisted suicide collected 112,500 signatures in a month." May we presume these intend

to be the first 112,500 people in line, or were they only being especially considerate of their fellow Hollanders? In the latter case, how generous they are in their civic courtesy.

"Supporters say it would offer a dignified way to die for those over 70 who just want to give up living, without having to resort to difficult or unreliable solitary suicide methods." Dignity is the overriding value. But it's good news that we will finally be done with those difficult suicide methods. The victim may have other things on his mind than whether the gas in the stove is on, or the rope sturdy enough. And good news, too, that we will be done with unreliable suicide methods. How embarrassing for a doctor to discover a failed medical procedure that accidentally leaves his patient dead, and how embarrassing to have a failed suicide procedure that accidentally leaves his patient alive.

"They might include widows and widowers overwhelmed by grief, those unwilling to face the frailties of extreme old age or people determined to 'get out while they're ahead' and meet death on their own terms." How long does Holland propose to give widows and widowers to decide if their grief is overwhelming? More than forty-eight hours, I hope. And it sounds as if one wins the game of life if one reaches the end without sorrow or suffering, but even so, do we admire the football team that quits in the third quarter because it is ahead?

"The assistants who administered the deadly cocktail of sedatives would need to be certified, campaigners said." What would the certification guarantee? Being reliable? Then if they say I'll be dead by Thursday, I'd better not see Friday's sunrise. Or is it a guarantee they won't use difficult methods, like bludgeoning me senseless with an iron pipe? And how do these certified practitioners advertise? Instead of ambulance chasers, will we find them hanging around nursing homes, or passing out their cards at Denny's 4:00 early bird senior supper special?

"But critics say there is scope for the elderly to come under untoward pressure from unscrupulous relatives." This brings to mind a thousand comical conversations at the Thanksgiving dinner table. "Come on, Dad, don't you think you've had enough turkey. And say, don't you think you've had enough of life? How long are you going to hang on to that property?"

"And the Royal Dutch Medical Association . . . fears patients would use the policy as a way of getting around their own doctors." Does this mean not paying their own doctors? Is that the real concern?

"Many religious groups oppose any form of suicide on principle." Glad the newspaper thought to mention it. And by the way, it's an opposition based on more than philosophical principle.

Only the sane person can laugh. Maybe boredom brings a person to the point of saying "I've had enough." If so, then Chesterton's words on suicide apply: "It is the ultimate and absolute evil, the refusal to take an interest in existence; the refusal to take the oath of loyalty to life. . . . The thief is satisfied with diamonds; but the suicide is not: that is his crime. He cannot be bribed, even by the blazing stones of the Celestial City." However, the problem in this case is not boredom, it is fear. And not even a wholesome, proper fear of death. Their greatest fear is to become helpless, to be reliant, to suffer, to become limited. Perhaps that's why Christians daily practice dying since their baptism. And imagine having no one over 70 to tell me what "see you in the funny papers" means.

THE ILLOGICAL BIKE RACK

'm going to tell an embarrassing tale on myself in order to identify the illogic that is the subject of this essay. In so doing, I am throwing myself on the mercy of my readers, hoping that they will not think too poorly of me. But I suspect they might remember some similar experience of their own that could even lead them to sympathize with me.

In our younger, more aerobic and adventuresome days, I attached a bike rack to the rear bumper of our automobile in case my wife and I were moved by some sudden urge to peddle a path that began far from home. What if the bike path was so far away that our two-wheeled transportation itself required transport to that place of exercise? We still bike today, but confine ourselves to the more immediate environs. But in those days I wished to stand prepared for the eventuality of bicycling through a pine forest in the northwest corner of the state, or alongside the meandering Mississippi, or through bucolic farmland. The fact that I cannot remember ever having made one of these tours does not remove the pride I still feel at having been ready, should we have ever wanted to.

The only annoyance caused by a bike rack on the rear bumper of an automobile is the hindrance it causes in accessing the trunk. Boxes and parcels which would have slid into the trunk with ease became a challenge when the opening was blocked by a rack in the middle. I can remember one particular day, the day penultimate to the end of this story, when I helped move someone from their apartment and worked up a sweat trying to insert a number of boxes into the trunk. That struggle fixed the impression in my mind that the bike rack was an obstacle to placing particularly large objects into the trunk. That is how it came to pass on the following day that I actually found myself saying out loud to my sister, who, after lunch downtown, suggested I could give her a lift home if I threw her bike into my car trunk: "I don't know if I can fit it in around the bike rack."

I reiterate my hope that the reader will moderate his chuckle over my illogic by recalling some illogical remark of his own, for I suppose it happens often enough, and innocently enough. Some object or event is so firmly impressed in her mind that we say something that translates into we can't accept the solution because it is in the way of the problem we're trying to solve. I can provide one more example, from a conversation with one of my college students whose grades were slipping. He didn't have time to study, he patiently explained, because he had to work; and he needed to work because he needed the money; and he needed the money to pay for his car; and the main reason he needed his car was to get to work.

Most commentators and biographers of Chesterton sooner or later get around to saying that he had a "penetrating mind." I think it might be better said that he had a "comprehending mind." His wisdom derived not so much from penetrating further into an argument already laid out, but instead from pausing to look up and ask why we are trying to fit the bike around the bike rack in the first place. By way of example, I offer his opposition to a bill in Parliament that proposed to do away with head lice in the slums by cutting short the hair of all the children in the slums. In Chesterton's opinion, Parliament was saying that because it is long and laborious to do away with dirty slums, it is preferable to do away with dirty hair, and the easiest way to accomplish that is to cut it off. Chesterton objected. He objected vehemently. Even violently.

> With the red hair of one she-urchin in the gutter I will set fire to all modern civilization. Because a girl should have long hair, she should have clean hair; because she should have clean hair, she should not have an unclean home; because she should not have an unclean home, she should have a free and leisured mother; because she should have a free mother, she should not have a usurious landlord; because there should not be an usurious landlord, there should be a redistribution of property, because there should be a redistribution of property, there shall be a revolution. That little urchin with the gold-red hair, whom I have just watched toddling past my house, she shall not be lopped and lamed and altered; her hair shall not be cut short like a convict's; no, all the kingdoms of the earth shall be hacked about and mutilated to suit her. She is the human and

sacred image; all around her the social fabric shall sway and split and fall; the pillars of society shall be shaken, and the roofs of ages come rushing down; and not one hair of her head shall be harmed.

I do not read this challenge as if Chesterton was behind his times for opposing women in the work place. I read it as if Chesterton was higher than his times—and ours—comprehending the illogic of saying the solution is in the way of our program.

COLD COMFORT

When one is in a Chestertonian frame of mind, all sorts of ordinary and idle comments, even ones made in innocence, can strike one as hilarious. And portentous. So it was in a radio interview I heard with a scientist who had secured funding to conduct experimentation that would splice DNA in such a way as to create a new microorganism. This was going to be "pure science," he reported gravely, intending to reassure the listener. After admitting under further examination that the innocent product in the Petri dish could conceivably be turned to less innocent uses, for example, biochemical warfare, he may have sensed that the listeners' initial comfort from knowing he was going to be doing pure science was ebbing. So he added this consolation: "it will take about another three years." He was trying to comfort me, but it was a cold comfort.

Imagine a spy counseling calm in Parliament because, although a barbarian force was amassing on the borders that made Genghis Khan look like a child at a tea party, and although this horde was making preparation to invade and pillage and murder, it would take at least three years for them to arrive.

Imagine a doctor, in a befuddled state of mind, confusing arsenic with aspirin and writing you the wrong prescription for your mild headache, but tossing the mistake lightly aside by reassuring you that the poisonous element is of such mild dosage that it will take at least three years to kill you.

Imagine how it would gladden the hearts of solicitous parents to remember that, although junior drinks 'til midnight and sleeps 'til noon, and has yet to find even one of his classrooms, they can raise their morale by reminding each other that the commencement exercises in which junior will not take part are three years away.

These would be cold comforts.

Chesterton wrote a book with a title that reads both like a sentence and a question: *What's Wrong with the World.* If you take the title as a question, the answer Chesterton repetitively gives is that "we do not ask what is right." We cannot say whether a road is the right road or the wrong road until we have paused to debate where it is we want to go. Chesterton has definite opinions about where the human race should want to go, but I will save that stage of the argument for another time. For the moment, he just wants us to see the propriety of questioning the value of what we're about to do in the next three years, or three days, or three minutes, before we do it. It would be cold comfort if I ring you up to say that I plan to punch you in the nose but it will take me three minutes to reach your house. Do you merit a punch in the nose, or not? Will such a thump be the act of a bully, or a knight liberating a princess in your cellar? These are the questions that interest Chesterton.

What's wrong with the world is not that there people in laboratories doing pure science; what's wrong is that there are not people in universities, churches, and parliaments doing fruitful philosophy. What's wrong with the world is that we do not conduct long and clarifying discussions about why we are doing what we are doing. And such discussions belong at the point where they are needed most: at the beginning. If your emperor commanded you to build him a building, you might prefer to have some idea about the use to which he will put it in order to know whether to design a school or a coliseum or a home or a jail. And you might like to have that information before you're three years into pouring the cement.

There was a scientist on a children's television show many years ago, with unruly hair, wearing a white lab coat, accompanied by a muppet dog who spoke to him in barks that only he could understand. In one episode, this scientist spent the whole show calamitously trying to sew a button onto a fried egg. First he froze the egg, then he used special thread, then he put some additives in the frying pan when he prepared the egg, but each experiment failed him. So the dog barked a short conversation with the scientist at this point. "Why am I trying to sew a button onto a fried egg?" the scientist repeated, for the benefit of the audience who did not speak dog language. "Why am I trying to do it? I don't even know *how* I am going to do it yet. How should I know *why* I am trying to do it?"

"Progress is a useless word," Chesterton said; "for progress takes for granted an already defined direction." Perhaps we are making progress. Perhaps pure science did finally unlock nature's vault of secrets about fried eggs, and perhaps it will yet unlock its secrets about new microorganisms. Perhaps it will take about three years. But one thing is certain: we should begin debate now on whether either buttons on fried eggs or a microorganism that can kill a million people is a good thing to have. Is it a human and humane and worthwhile thing to have? That's all Chesterton wants to know.

ON BEING EDUCATED

Chesterton was a man of letters. By that I do not mean he spent his life in the ivory tower, since he spent it on the sidewalks of Fleet Street. What I mean is that he was a man of *words*. Words mattered to him. He listened carefully to words, wherever those words were spoken, even on the top of an omnibus, he confessed, where people spoke about such theological profundities as original sin without even knowing that was their subject.

The other day I listened to one word carefully, too, though it was not atop an omnibus (which do not frequent my neighborhood), it was in a committee meeting (which do frequent my schedule). As the word floated by, I cocked my head and pricked up my ears like the man of letters Chesterton was teaching me to be. The speaker was extolling the virtue of students studying abroad. She was committed to the cause of international education, and made her point with such fervor that I'm sure she didn't realize the gaffe it contained. In enumerating the benefits of studying abroad, she pointed out how valuable it is for someone "to spend time in another country where they can experience different cultures, different lifestyles, different moralities."

My ear twitched. I should find it interesting to visit such a place, myself, I thought. Last summer I had been in France, and, come to think of it, I had noticed a different culture. The bread was baked in a long and crusty form that was fun to tear apart; the Metro was efficient and easy; the shops contained more choices of cheese than I have seen in all my life. Yes, it was a more relaxed and gustatory culture than I experience here. And I noticed a different lifestyle. People spent time lazing at a sidewalk café table; the action had not moved from downtown to a French Mall anchored by a Wal-Mart; and I watched parents take time out to play soccer . . . excuse me, football, with their children in the park. Yes, it was a different lifestyle.

But I wondered how much further than France I would have to travel in order to find a people that kept a different morality.

Perhaps there is a place on the planet where our students can go to study where parents diligently teach their children how to lie. Either mother or father (whichever has mastered the art more expertly) sits junior down to explain the best ways to pervert the truth. Or perhaps a society can be found where spinelessness is saluted and there are tickertape parades in honor of cowards. Or perhaps thievery is so respected in some rural regions that people name their buildings after bandits and their kittens after cat burglars. Or perhaps families take weekly trips to the uncle's house in order to school the children in sloth and lechery so they will know how to put these morals into practice when their capacities mature. Or perhaps we could find a community smitten by vaingloriousness, holding envy in esteem, and admiring of avarice.

It seems unlikely to me, though. It seems far more likely to me that we would find a common morality expressed in different ways. This is a distinction C. S. Lewis makes in *Mere Christianity* where he says the universal rule must not be confused with particular social customs.

> The Christian rule of chastity must not be confused with the social rule of "modesty" (in one sense of that word); that is, propriety, or decency. The social rule of propriety lays down how much of the human body should be displayed and what subjects can be referred to, and in what words, according to the customs of a given social circle. Thus, while the rule of chastity is the same for all Christians at all times, the rule of propriety changes. A girl in the Pacific islands wearing hardly any clothes and a Victorian lady completely covered in clothes might both be equally "modest," proper, or decent, according to the standards of their own societies: and both, for all we could tell by their dress, might be equally chaste (or unchaste).

Chesterton thought morality was the cost of a conditional joy. We're intended for the same joy, so the same cost is laid on us all. It is the same in a domestic syllabus or an international syllabus, because it is on the syllabus of life. He defended it when dueling (verbally) with a fellow art student he calls simply The Diabolist.

"Aren't those sparks splendid?" I said.

"Yes," he replied.

"That is all that I ask you to admit," said I. "Give me those few red specks and I will deduce Christian morality. Once I thought like you, that one's pleasure in a flying spark was a thing that could come and go with that spark. Once I thought that the delight was as free as the fire. . . . But now I know that the red star is only on the apex of an invisible pyramid of virtues. That red fire is only the flower on a stalk of living habits, which you cannot see. . . . Seduce a woman, and that spark will be less bright. Shed blood, and that spark will be less red."

Now, it would be worth going to the ends of the earth to learn that lesson. Except we don't have to. We learn it in our hearts.

GRANDPA GILBERT'S LONG MEMORY

One of the things grandparents do is keep a history for the family. When the children think the snowfall is bad, grandma remembers the year they couldn't see the cow under the snow bank. When the parents think their children are bad, grandpa remembers what little dickens they were themselves. Grandparents put things in perspective by putting things into a historical picture.

Grandpa Gilbert liked to play this role, too. His own reading spanned eras, and he was familiar with Egyptians and Carthaginians and pagan Rome and Catholic Rome. When he became familiar with that last tribe, his vision was increased tenfold, for he describes the Church as "the only continuous intelligent institution that has been thinking about thinking for two thousand years." As a result, "a Catholic has fifty times more feeling of being free" because a Catholic "has the range of two thousand years of twelve-hundred thousand controversies, thrashed out by thinker against thinker." This means that Grandpa Gilbert is not easily impressed by one of modernity's favorite arguments, the argument that something is good if it is new. It may not be new.

Take birth control, for instance. There exist a few shadowy associations that lead most of us to think this is a relatively new possibility dropped into our lap by the gods of science from their lab on high. The vague image we possess of an ancient Roman citizen or archaic Medieval monk never has them wearing a lab coat, or peering into a microscope, or stirring things together in a test tube, and so we consider birth control something of which they were ignorant but we are blessed with by the grace of science. Lacking pharmacies with little white pills, the ancient and medieval mother-to-be was subject to brute nature, whereas we live in the radiant light of science rolling back the frontier of ignorance about where babies come from.

Grandpa Gilbert eases into his rocking chair and summons up a memory. What is quaintly called Birth Control, he begins, "is in fact a scheme for preventing birth in order to escape control." If we examine the phrase without its euphemistic coloring, it might more accurately be called "Birth Prevention," and it might be more practiced with more accuracy. For the ultimate goal is to prevent the birth of the sort of babies someone doesn't want, and

> if there is no authority in things which Christendom has called moral . . . then they are clearly free to ignore all difference between animals and men; and treat men as we treat animals. . . . The obvious course for Eugenists is to act towards babies as they act towards kittens. Let all the babies be born; and then let us drown those we do not like. I cannot see any objection to it; except the moral or mystical sort of objection that we advance against Birth-Prevention.

Grandpa Gilbert is recalling that this was the practice in ancient Rome. Let the baby be born, presented to the father, and if the father did not acknowledge it, the child was left to die. In a study of Christianity in the ancient world, entitled *The Rise of Christianity*, sociologist Rodney Stark records this letter from a man named Hilarion to his pregnant wife Alis. "Know that I am still in Alexandria. . . . If you are delivered of a child [before I come home], if it is a boy keep it, if a girl discard it. You have sent me word, 'Don't forget me.' How can I forget you. I beg you not to worry." Stark summarizes other studies, citing one at Delphi that enabled researchers to reconstruct six hundred families, and of these only six had raised more than one daughter. He explains, "Exposure of unwanted female infants and deformed male infants was legal, morally accepted, and widely practiced by all social classes in the Greco-Roman world." Both Plato and Aristotle recommended infanticide as legitimate state policy, and the earliest known Roman legal code permitted a father to expose any female infant, and any deformed or weak male infant. Stark also devotes a chapter to the practice of another kind of birth prevention, recorded in Tertullian's description in AD 203 of an abortion kit used by Hippocrates, the man who is the very source of the Hippocratic oath to protect and preserve life.

What goes around, comes around. Sociologists have calculated that in ancient Italy there were 140 males to 100 females. There are reports from China today—under headlines that read "China grapples with legacy of its 'missing girls'"—that the ratio there is 120 males to 100 females, rising steadily since 1990. The imbalance is accounted for by the combination of three factors: a state-enforced policy of only one child, the preference for a male child, and inexpensive ultra-sounds provided by portable scanners that allow prenatal sex selection.

Since the Catholic Church opposes birth control, the Catholic Church is assumed to be against progress, against advancement, against making life easier through science and chemistry. That is not it at all. Rather, when one has the perspective afforded by two thousand years of twelve-hundred thousand controversies, one sees where certain ideas lead, and down some of those paths we would do well to refrain from going. Grandpa Gilbert would have us realize that the Church does not hold its position because it is backward, behind the times, slow-witted; it holds its position because in every age it presses forward the moral and mystical basis for the dignity of every human being.

A PATRIOT OF THE SEXES

Chesterton operated with a kind of patriotism that was exclusive of imperialism. He was proud of Britain, but this did not mean he thought all the French should become British. To use other words he sometimes employed, he preferred being international to being cosmopolitan. "All good men are international. Nearly all bad men are cosmopolitan." The internationalist knows there are two separate and different nations that should have relations with one another; the cosmopolitan thinks he should be a little bit of every nation while not actually being a citizen of any one. "The more a man really appreciates and admires the soul of another people the less he will attempt to imitate it; he will be conscious that there is something in it too deep and too unmanageable to imitate." I suppose Chesterton wanted the French to remain French for the reason that he could then have French bread along with his English muffins. He did not hunger for a bland, cosmopolitan white bread baked from the same recipe in every bakery of Europe. There can be two good things.

Now I think that this is the only way to understand certain remarks Chesterton makes about the sexes. He says things about men that are certain to be misconstrued as politically incorrect until you realize that by saying them he doesn't mean that women are wrong for not being like men. He is a patriot of his male sex, but he is not an imperialist who thinks women should be more like men; even less is he a cosmopolitan who thinks the two sexes should become increasingly alike and undifferentiated. "I do not think there is anyone who takes quite such fierce pleasure in things being themselves as I do. The startling wetness of water excites and intoxicates me: the fieriness of fire, the steeliness of steel, the unutterable muddiness of mud. It is just the same with people. . . . When we call a man 'manly' or a woman 'womanly' we touch the deepest philosophy." I shall present two connected examples to illustrate my point.

First, Chesterton thinks men and women generally do not speak the same way. "Women speak to each other; men speak to the subject they are speaking about." Chesterton is saying this patriotically, and he is proud of the man's mode of conversation, even as he appreciates the woman's mode of conversation. He can be patriotically proud of the English weather even as he better appreciates France's warmer climate. It's the way England is, and it's the way men are, and he's proud of both.

"Many an honest man has sat in a ring of his five best friends under heaven and forgotten who was in the room while he explained some system. This is not peculiar to intellectual men; men are all theoretical, whether they are talking about God or golf. Men are all impersonal . . . every man speaks to a visionary multitude; a mystical cloud, that is called the club. It is obvious that this cool and careless quality which is essential to the collective affection of males involves disadvantages and dangers. It leads to spitting; it leads to coarse speech." If men speak to the subject and not to each other, as women do, then men's relationship with each other will never reach the depth or intensity it does between women. And we will need two different words to describe two different kinds of relationships. "Comradeship is at the most only one half of human life; the other half is Love, a thing so different that one might fancy it had been made for another universe. And I do not mean mere sex love; any kind of concentrated passion, maternal love, or even the fiercer kinds of friendship are in their nature alien to pure comradeship."

The second example is related to the first because its existence is a consequence of the first. The club exists as a place to engage this manner of speech. The man's club is a place for camaraderie and tomfoolery and, as Chesterton noted, spitting. But there must be a place more intimate than the club, just as there must be a relationship more affectionate than comradeship. Chesterton has in mind the home, where love prevails. And he does not doubt which is the superior, any more than he doubts that French sun is preferable to the English fog. But, damn it, a patriot will defend even the English damp, and a man will even defend his club.

> Both sides are essential to life; and both are known in differing degrees to everybody of every age or sex. But very broadly speaking it may still be said that women stand for the dignity of love and men for the dignity of comradeship. I mean that

the institution would hardly be expected if the males of the tribe did not mount guard over it. The affections in which women excel have so much more authority and intensity that pure comradeship would be washed away if it were not rallied and guarded in clubs, corps, colleges, banquets and regiments. Most of us have heard the voice in which the hostess tells her husband not to sit too long over the cigars. It is the dreadful voice of Love, seeking to destroy Comradeship.

NAKED NONSENSE

T he answer to the question of whether nakedness is natural would, of course, depend somewhat upon what one thought of nakedness, but more importantly upon what one thought of as natural. If natural meant "the way something is without interference," then, yes, one must concede that naked babies are natural; or if natural meant pre-civilized, brute nature, akin to animals, then we would again concede that in his unclothed state the baby has more in common with a baboon than does the gentleman in top hat and tux. But if natural means normal, and normal is the expression of a norm or standard, then we might make a distinction between nudity and nakedness, and question the naturalness of the latter.

C. S. Lewis first called this to my attention in *The Four Loves* where he points out that "The word naked was originally a past participle; the naked man was the man who had undergone a process of naking, that is, of stripping or peeling (you used the verb of nuts and fruits)." His remark made me hear the word in a new way. If I have a thirst, and slake it, then my thirst has been slaked; if I am going too fast in an automobile and depress the middle peddle, then I have braked; and Adam and Eve were normal and nude, until they sinned and realized they were naked. Chesterton remarks, "there is nothing the matter with the human body; what is the matter is with the human soul." That is why, Lewis continues, "Time out of mind the naked man has seemed to our ancestors not the natural but the abnormal man; not the man who has abstained from dressing but the man who has been for some reason undressed."

It is a challenge for the modern reader to even pronounce the word in question as one syllable, but make the effort to do so in order to hear a different grammar. Pronounce it as one syllable, like snaked or raked or staked. Woe the person who has been naked, who is a piece of nature instead of a part of society. His nakedness (two syllables, not three) is a glaring sign of his isolation from the human clan. Wearing no clothes woven by a guild of weavers out of products supplied by a band of shepherds or community of farmers, the person who has been naked stands alone, unrelated, solitarily. He is an individual of a species, but not a person, for he wears no mask (persona) to indicate his place in the larger social world. He carries no sign of social responsibility upon his head, and has no personal history draping from his shoulders. He has no ties or buttons or fasteners to bind him to an obligation or relationship; he has no pockets in which to place treasures discovered during a walkabout. Solitary, disconnected by mores or civility, unhindered, we are most assuredly not our true selves when we are naked, because our true self is a construct, a task, a history, a person(ality).

Chesterton said the modern world has reached the curious condition of continuing to do sensible things without having any of the sensible reasons for doing them, and chooses two examples to make his point in *The Roots of Sanity*. One is the sensible state of being clothed; the other is the sensible practice of not eating each other. "Most of our friends and acquaintances continue to entertain a healthy prejudice against Cannibalism. . . . But the *reason* for disapproving of cannibalism has already become very vague. It remains as a tradition and an instinct." He thinks this a very odd situation for a modern world lectures everyone in hearing distance on the deadness of tradition. Yet here it is, refraining from Adamitism (nudity) and Anthropophagy (eating of flesh) not on principle but on prejudice alone.

But not everywhere. "We have seen the New Adamite or No Clothes Movement start quite seriously in Germany; start indeed with a seriousness of which only Germans are capable. Englishmen probably are still English enough to laugh at it and dislike it. But they laugh by instinct; and they only dislike by instinct. Most of them, with their present muddled moral philosophy, would probably have great difficulty in refuting the Prussian professor of nakedness." He worries that the same defenseless condition might then apply in the case of the theory of cannibalism. One would think that "a banker walking down the street with no clothes on" would be quite as nonsensical as "a butcher selling man instead of mutton," but Chesterton is concerned that the number of people who could explain why is shrinking.

May we be satisfied to merely hope that prejudices will continue? Are habits strong enough to hold the weight? Is tradition alone enough to keep a society clothed, and man out of the meat market? I was tempted by Chesterton's remark to take recourse to the web, and yes, there is the case of "German cannibal Armin Meiwes in 2006" who very seriously ate a man who answered his ad, noting at the time of his prosecution that the country of Germany, like other Western nations, had no law prohibiting cannibalism. Chesterton's point is that "the modern theorist will have to defend his own sanity with a prejudice. It is the mediaeval theologian who can defend it with a reason."

It was once traditional to revere life, battle death, honor our promises, not shoot our schoolmates, and so forth. We stand naked, without principles, left to rely on social sanities that are but the traditions of old dogmas. "Like many other Catholic dogmas, they are felt in some vague way even by heathens, so long as they are healthy heathens. . . . They have the prejudice; and long may they retain it! We have the principle, and they are welcome to it when they want it."

A SHORT HISTORY OF TRADE AND INDUSTRY DURING THE NINETEENTH AND EARLY TWENTIETH CENTURIES

This is the longest title that I have ever placed on my column, but it comes directly from the pen of Chesterton, as does the history itself, which is surprisingly terse. It goes: there was a man who sold razors, "and afterwards explained to an indignant customer, with simple dignity, that he had never said the razors would shave. When asked if razors were not made to shave, he replied that they were made to sell. That is A Short History of Trade and Industry During the Nineteenth and Early Twentieth Centuries." Allow a brief unpacking of the point.

Chesterton identified a soured paradox in the odor that wafts our way from this short history. The paradox is: the more we produce, the less we possess. "We live today in a world of witchcraft, in which the orchards wither because they prosper, and the multitude of apples on the apple-tree of itself turns them into forbidden fruit, and makes the effort to consume them in every sense fruitless. This is the modern economic paradox, which is called Over-Production, or a glut in the market . . ." and it is unnatural indeed. It is as if an Irishman had said "they starved because the potatoes were gigantic and innumerable."

This modern economic paradox is more miraculous than a miracle, for if we are told in the Gospels that a few loaves and fishes were multiplied, we could safely conclude that more people were fed; "no creed or dogma ever declared that there was too little food because there was too much fish." This is more fantastic than a fairy tale, for "it is one thing to believe that a beanstalk scaled the sky, and quite another to believe that fifty-seven beans make five." Something very strange, indeed, has been going on during the Short History of Trade and Industry During the Nineteenth and Early Twentieth Centuries. It is a magical, mystical mathematic in which more means less.

I recently had reason to think of the man selling razors. The following story is an unembellished account straight from the front page of the major Chicago newspaper, so you know it is true. I have held myself to as little commentary as I can resist. It seems that there is a company in the city whose purpose was thought by many to be providing energy for people's homes. It was called "Peoples Energy," which is what led many to this conclusion. This company "transferred or sold natural gas intended to heat Chicagoans' homes to a venture of its parent company and Enron Corporation," with the unforeseen consequence that "the utility was forced to replenish gas supplies at high prices on the open market," which resulted in record heating bills for customers.

For those of us unfamiliar with the natural gas trade, the newspaper pauses to explain the fundamental principles. "Utilities try to keep customers' bills low by buying natural gas at cheaper prices in the summer, when it is in lower demand. They then release the gas in the winter when consumers need it to heat their homes." I am with them so far. But documents show "that over a three year period, Peoples Gas transferred or sold at least 128 billion cubic feet of gas a year [40% of its storage capacity] to Enron Midwest." I shall not be sidetracked from my main point by going into the fact that Enron Midwest "was secretly sharing profits on gas trading with a company called Enovate, an unregulated joint venture of Enron and Peoples Energy." My main point is that while these deals generated $10.5 million in profit for Peoples Energy, "Peoples Gas had to buy replacement gas when prices peaked in the winter of 2000-01 and then passed those higher costs on to customers." What else could they do, since consumers pay for the gas? Heating bills were about double what they had been the year before.

So there is another Short History of Trade and Industry During the Nineteenth and Early Twentieth Centuries. There was a man who sold natural gas. One day in court he had to explain to an indignant attorney general and Citizens' Utility Board, who seemed unreasonably upset, that he never said natural gas was to heat people's homes and fuel their stoves. When asked whether the whole reason for natural gas was to not make a warm sanctuary from the Chicago winds and to heat the children's cocoa, he replied, with some mild surprise, that he thought natural gas was made to sell.

Place this manager in charge of the orchard, Chesterton suggests, and he will not look upon apples as things to eat, but as things to sell. He will not produce as many apples as he plans to eat, but as many apples as he hopes to sell, and if his neighbor does the same "they will produce so many apples that apples in the market will be about as valuable as pebbles on the beach. Thus each of them will find he has very little money in his pocket, with which to go and buy fresh pears at the fruiterer's shop." And that is a Short History of something other than Distributism at work During the Nineteenth and Early Twentieth Centuries.

PART 4
Catholicism

"As human institutions go, the Church was not peculiar in having evils, but peculiar in admitting them."
March 14, 1908

GETTING PRACTICAL

One of the advantages of speaking a living language is that you often get twice the meaning for your money. For a time, at least, until it fades away, the original grammar of a word provides one meaning, while the new and commonly accepted grammar provides another. I am thinking of a particular case in point.

In popular grammar, the word "practically" has come to mean "almost," and I provide three examples for illustration:

(a) She taught me practically everything I know;

(b) I am practically finished;

(c) I'm practically married.

The connotation of this word in ordinary language means almost, virtually, all but, basically, nearly, or just about in the state being described. Thus I would be understood to be saying (a) I learned almost everything from her, (b) I'm nearly finished, and (c) any day now I'm on the verge of marrying.

One receives a very different feeling if one looks at the word from a stricter rule structure. When the suffix "-ly" is affixed to a word it adds the sense of "has the characteristics of." It affirms that something is like, or resembles, the state named by the word without the suffix. So "efficiently" means done in an efficient manner, and "beautifully" means done in a beautiful way, and, by this stricter rule, "practically" means done in a way that is practical. It refers to that which has to do with practice instead of theory, that which is learned through action instead of speculation. It relates to what is concretely manifested. It is concerned with production or operation or putting into effect.

This gives a rather different meaning to the three sentences I proposed two paragraphs above. The sentences now mean (a) Fr. Kavanagh taught me everything I theoretically know about liturgy but Sharon taught me how to commit liturgy; (b) After weeks of thinking about this article, I have put pen to paper and now it exists; (c) I am not in love with the idea of being married, I am in love with Elizabeth and our marriage has a concrete consequence upon everything I do and think and am. So, apparently (that is, in a way that is apparent), the meaning of the word "practically" has sauntered slowly from "in a way that is practical" to "for all practical purposes" to "all but; nearly; almost."

Now, with this distinction in mind, I think it could be said about Chesterton that he was practically a husband, practically a writer, practically a romantic, and practically a Distributist.

The reader who has been following attentively will know I do not mean Chesterton was almost a married author whose wild ideas about redistributing wealth came to naught. I mean that he was a husband who approved of marriage not just in theory but in his very personal case. And he did not, like so many aspiring bus boys in Hollywood, fancy himself a writer—he actually made a living with his pen. And his romantic view of life extended beyond utopian dreams to an actual lifestyle with liberties he thought bohemians could only dream about. And his theories about human happiness were not merged with theories debated in Parliament or among German philosophers, they were put at the service of the charwoman and the green grocer.

I am also interested in the fact that, unlike many on the American scene today, Chesterton was practically religious. I remember being startled by what Chesterton had found startling about the future Mrs. Chesterton when she was still Frances Blogg.

> [She had] a sort of hungry appetite for all the fruitful things like fields and gardens and anything connected with production; about which she was quite practical. She practised gardening; in that curious cockney culture she would have been quite ready to practise farming; and on the same perverse principle, she actually practised a religion. This was something utterly unaccountable both to me and to the whole fussy culture in which she lived. Any number of people proclaimed religions, chiefly oriental religions, analysed or argued about them; but that anybody could regard religion as a practical thing like gardening was something quite new to me and, to her neighbors, new and incomprehensible.

The pollsters tell me that when it comes to religion, Americans would rather believe than practice. A religion with obligations is a bit too confining; a religion with nothing but ideals would be ideal. To think about the divine almost every week is less intrusive than being expected to come to God's house, practically, every week. Religion as a theory is easier than religion as a practice.

Chesterton had a broader view. He did not deny that religion conditioned people's theories, but he added that religion practically taught man, too.

> Religion, the immortal maiden, has been a maid-of-all-work as well as a servant of mankind. She provided men at once with the theoretic laws of an unalterable cosmos; and also with the practical rules of the rapid and thrilling game of morality. She taught logic to the student and told fairy tales to the children; it was her business to confront the nameless gods whose fears are on all flesh, and also to see the streets were spotted with silver and scarlet, that there was a day for wearing ribbons or an hour for ringing bells.

Believing thus, Chesterton practically became a Catholic.

WISHING YOU A
VULGAR CHRISTMAS

According to some secret and infallible knowledge that magazine editors possess about the working of time, I am informed that although the deadline for a next submission to *Gilbert!* falls in the middle of autumn, when our thoughts will be fixed on apples and pumpkins and colored leaves, such submission should be "tailored to the Christmas season where possible." That means that although as these words are being written there is still no sign of tinsel, trees or toys, said editor predicts that as these words are read we shall be sick to death of televised specials starring Santa, Rudolph or Frosty.

Perhaps by the time these words are read, some of us will have even begun clucking our tongues and wagging our heads in disgust at the vulgar accouterments that have attached themselves to the feast of the Nativity. Complaining about the excesses will become a favorite way to begin conversation in certain societies. We will note that the window displays are even gaudier this year, we will remember when stores used to wait until after Thanksgiving to begin advertising, some might suggest putting Christ back in Christmas. This caviling will be variously inspired; I can think of three motivators. The temperate person will think the feasting and drinking has gotten out of hand. Highbrows will think it preferable to give a nod of approval to the idea behind the feast, rather than slump into actual participation. And some puritans will object that the theology of the Christmas feast could be better preserved without corruption from pagan profanities. However, on the basis of remarks Chesterton makes about Christmas, I'm inclined to believe that instead of joining any of these three types of nigglers, we will instead find him stringing the garland and basting the goose.

First, the temperate spirit strives for moderation, acting to avoid both want and excess; it therefore finds both the Christmas feast and the Lenten fast puzzling. Chesterton believes such puzzlement might serve as an expansive stumbling block for that soul, so leaves the conundrum untouched.

> When the anxious ethical inquirer says, "Christmas is devoted to merry-making, to eating meat and drinking wine, and yet you encourage this pagan and materialistic enjoyment," you or I will be tempted to say, "Quite right, my boy," and leave it at that. When he then says, looking even more worried, "Yet you admire men for fasting in caves and deserts and denying themselves ordinary pleasures; you are clearly committed, like the Buddhists, to the opposite or ascetic principle," we shall be similarly inspired to say, "Quite correct, old bean," or "Got it the first time, old top," and merely propose an adjournment for convivial refreshment.

Chesterton makes no attempt to explain matters until the temperate mind has been sufficiently expanded to see that human well-being is served by both conditions.

Second, the highbrow approves of Christmas in general, and feasting in theory, and has a certain distant appreciation of historic festive rituals, but has a difficult time loosening his own collar and joining in. Chesterton was surrounded by such people in his day. They liked to talk about the glories of ancient festivals, but

> there is about these people a haunting and alarming something which suggests that it is just possible that they don't keep Christmas. It is painful to regard human nature in such a light, but it seems somehow possible that Mr. George Moore does not wave his spoon and shout when the pudding is set alight. It is even possible that Mr. W. B. Yeats never pulls crackers. If so, where is the sense of all their dreams of festive traditions? Here is a solid and ancient festive tradition still plying a roaring trade in the streets, and they think it vulgar. If this be so, let them be very certain of this, that they are the kind of people who in the time of the maypole would have thought the maypole vulgar; who in the time of the Canterbury pilgrimage would have thought the Canterbury pilgrimage vulgar; who in the time of

the Olympian games would have thought the Olympian games vulgar. Nor can there be any reasonable doubt that they were vulgar. . . . Vulgarity there always was wherever there was joy, wherever there was faith in the gods. . . . If we ever get the English back on to the English land they will become again a religious people, if all goes well, a superstitious people.

To sophisticates, the word "vulgar" means deficient in taste, delicacy, or refinement; marked by a lack of good breeding; boorish. To Chesterton the word means what it originally meant—belonging to the common people—whose company he enjoyed very much.

Third, Puritan objections stem from a prejudice against any trappings that seem pagan. A partial list of offenses associated with Christmas would include pine trees, Yule logs, mistletoe, and even the December date because it is supposed to derive from the Teutonic winter solstice. In order to be Christian, they think, the celebration must discard any festive embellishments also utilized by non-christians. To Chesterton, this is baffling. To complain that Christmas feasts or processions or dances are of pagan origin is like saying "that our legs are of pagan origin. Nobody ever disputed that humanity was human before it was Christian; and no Church manufactured the legs with which men walked or danced, either in a pilgrimage or a ballet. What can really be maintained, so as to carry not a little conviction, is this: that where such a Church has existed it has preserved not only the processions but the dances; not only the cathedral but the carnival." Far from being dismayed over some commonality between the Christian Christmas and the pagan festival, Chesterton is pleased that the former seems to fulfill and preserve the latter. "All that genuinely remains of the ancient hymns or the ancient dances of Europe, all that has honestly come to us from the festivals of Phoebus or Pan, is to be found in the festivals of the Christian Church. If any one wants to hold the end of a chain which really goes back to the heathen mysteries, he had better take hold of a festoon of flowers at Easter or a string of sausages at Christmas." Chesterton is very happy to discover that the hearth fire in a stable on the outskirts of Bethlehem has a kinship to the fires round which pagan antiquity built human civilization. "There is nothing quite like this warmth, as in the warmth of Christmas, amid ancient hills hoary with such snows of antiquity. It can address even God Almighty with diminutives."

Chesterton will rescue my Christmas when it comes. I will be tempted to look critically at a Christian holy day become an Americanized holiday. But Chesterton will remind me that the divine warmth that smothered the world in the darkest night of the year is a warmth that can be felt from the celebration even before it was learned by the seeker.

> Any agnostic or atheist whose childhood has known a real Christmas has ever afterwards, whether he likes it or not, an association in his mind between two ideas that most of mankind must regard as remote from each other; the idea of a baby and the idea of unknown strength that sustains the stars. His instincts and imagination can still connect them, when his reason can no longer see the need of the connection; for him there will always be some savour of religion about the mere picture of a mother and a baby; some hint of mercy and softening about the mere mention of the dreadful name of God. But the two ideas are not naturally or necessarily combined. . . . It is no more inevitable to connect God with an infant than to connect gravitation with a kitten. It has been created in our minds by Christmas because we are Christians; because we are psychological Christians even when we are not theological ones.

NOT SO MERRY CHRISTMAS

When I look over the Christmas essays I have done, it seems that I have usually focused on Chesterton's childlike delight in the celebration. His more sophisticated neighbors seem perplexed, and he seems delighted. They are accustomed to a plain, puritan, abstract religion, and Chesterton hangs tinsel from their hats and puts a cup of wassail in their hands. But I have thought of another class of persons perplexed by Christmas, though in a different way. Chesterton was equally deft at unsettling them. A taxonomist might seek to classify them for ease of recognition, the way one would classify a group of forest ferns or sea snails for easy recognition, and he might propose the scientific name of *Herodianus Sui Sovereignus* for these people.

There once was a king who went to great lengths to protect himself from Christmas. If this were a fairy tale, you might imagine this nasty king going to such extremes as declaring that the Royal Post Office must burn any cards that arrive to his kingdom. He forbids his subjects to make any special recognition of their neighbor on the street, and insists they pass by each other with sober eye and grim countenance. For the duration of those unmentionable twelve days, he outlaws the colors red, white, purple, silver—well, in fact, any color but grey. He cuts down all the fir trees in a fifty mile radius so that no one can put up a tree, and sends his minions to cut the toes out of all the stockings in the department store so that no one can hang one upon the fireplace mantle. In a fairy tale, that is how a king might seek to protect himself from Christmas.

Unfortunately, life can be even harsher than fairy tales, and real kings can be more grim than the Brothers Grimm ever imagined. There once was a king who went to such lengths to protect himself from Christmas that he ordered not cards burned or trees felled, but babies killed. This king thought he was protecting his power. Now, it was true that he did possess a degree of power, but it was only on loan to him from the high king. It was a gift granted for service. And now there were rumors that the high king was coming for an accounting (and when one is protecting a spurious position, one is especially susceptible to rumors). What this king had been granted as a gift he had arrogated as a possession, and now he was getting nervous, so he decided to act.

This circumstance made the first Christmas a rather sneaky business. Most Christmases since that one have been gaudy and public events, held openly in the streets and town squares. But this first Christmas was a real cloak-and-dagger affair, literally so, considering the daggers the soldiers hid beneath their cloaks as they entered Bethlehem. At the first Christmas, the high king had to come undercover. Indeed, Chesterton points out, he came underground. "By the very nature of the story the rejoicings in the cavern were rejoicings in a fortress or an outlaw's den; properly understood it is not unduly flippant to say they were rejoicings in a dug-out." The first Christmas was a furtive affair, worthy of an adventure tale wherein the true king of England was smuggled across the channel under a load of fish. Chesterton envisions the Creator stooping so low as to be smuggled into his own creation. It is an undignified position for the high king, but he seems only all too willing to adopt it if this is how he must enter enemy territory. Regrettably, our own hearts are too often that territory.

More than smuggling, it was an actual attack. The high king was coming to balance the books and demand an account. The false king would be asked whether his sovereignty-on-loan was being used for the good of his citizens, or only to his own gain. That is why Christmas was an unsettling affair for him and his type.

> It is not only that the very horse-hoofs of Herod might in that sense have passed like thunder over the sunken head of Christ. It is also that there is in that image a true idea of an outpost, of a piercing through the rock and an entrance into an enemy territory. There is in this buried divinity an idea of undermining the world; of shaking the towers and palaces from below; even as Herod the great king felt the earthquake under him and swayed with his swaying palace.

Not only does Christmas upset the puritan for being too pagan, and the theosophist for being too mundane, Christmas also upsets the mighty who mistakenly think they possess their wealth or power for their own self-gratification. The gifts that are on loan are to be put in service to the high king, who commands them exercised with a preferential option for the poor. Such types as I have been trying to classify not only occupy a palace in Jerusalem, but also a board room on Wall Street, and a back hallway in Washington. As I look around the landscape of my own world, I think the Christmas rumors that the Messiah is afoot must cause the same consternation in many.

LEGGISHNESS

I have confirmed, by experimental methods I would not like to recommend to anyone else or like to repeat again myself, a fact that I suspected about myself, namely, that I make a lousy patient. After dealing with a degenerative hip condition for the past five years, I underwent hip replacement surgery a year ago, and now have a steel ball and cup that will set off airport alarms from here to Kalamazoo. I was assured that eventually I would be scampering around like a squirrel, challenging small children to foot races and winning handily, but I was not confident of that while I was pushing a walker around the house. And I learned by first-hand experience that Norwegian stoicism is not of the whiny variety. It is an isolating type of stoicism that does not want aid or succor from even the most selfless souls, which puts my wife (who I am describing) in an awkward position. I learned why God did not give to men any of the hard things or painful things to do.

Chesterton was once on crutches with a sprained ankle, and I don't know what kind of patient he made for Frances, but he did spin fate's straw into philosophical gold in an essay entitled "The Advantages of Having One Leg." "I sing with confidence because I have recently been experimenting in the poetic pleasures which arise from having to sit in one chair with a sprained foot, with the only alternative course of standing on one leg like a stork—a stork is a poetic simile; therefore I eagerly adopted it." (I am reminded of a joke from my elementary school days. Q: why does the flamingo stand on one leg? A: Because if he tucked it under his wing, too, he'd fall down.)

What is the lesson Chesterton learned? "To appreciate anything we must always isolate it," and he gives some examples. "One sun is splendid; six suns would be only vulgar." It is possible not only to have too few, but also too many, and the isolation of the thing can remind one of when the arithmetic is just right. "One Tower Of Giotto is sublime; a row of Towers of Giotto would be only like a row of white posts. The poetry of art is in beholding the single tower; the poetry of nature in seeing the single tree; the poetry of love in following the single woman; the poetry of religion in worshipping the single star." This was 1909, before his Catholic days, or else I am sure he would have also added that the poetry of religion is in worshipping only one God.

But the poetic realization must lead to a moral conclusion that takes root in the realm of the virtues. There are plenty of contingencies that cause us to realize something intellectually. The question is whether the mind will ever descend to the heart, and sometimes misfortune nudges it along. "This world and all our powers in it are far more awful and beautiful than even we know until some accident reminds us. If you wish to perceive that limitless felicity, limit yourself if only for a moment."

It seems that all of life was a religious occasion for Chesterton. He pities the modern man or woman who finds nothing more than an accident in an accident, whereas he finds that an accident can remind us of something awful and beautiful. My distressed hip could serve as a theophany to me as easily as Jacob's hip served him after the angel dislocated it with the touch of a fingertip, were I capable of it. Building that capacity for gratitude is an accomplishment. So Chesterton concludes, "I feel grateful for the slight sprain which has introduced this mysterious and fascinating division between one of my feet and the other. The way to love anything is to realise that it might be lost. In one of my feet I can feel how strong and splendid a foot is; in the other I can realise how very much otherwise it might have been. The moral of the thing is wholly exhilarating."

Temporarily lose something, and you can finally stop taking it for granted. The abnormal state is the only thing that prevents us from taking the normal state for granted. The secret to religious gratitude is seeing all things with such eyes. When Chesterton did, then he saw "that life was as precious as it was puzzling. It was an ecstasy because it was an adventure; it was an adventure because it was an opportunity. . . . The test of all happiness is gratitude; and I felt grateful, though I hardly knew to whom. Children are grateful when Santa Claus puts in their stockings gifts of toys or sweets. Could I not be grateful to Santa Claus when he put in my stockings the gift of two miraculous legs?"

But just like children who eventually come to know it is their parents, not Santa Claus, who fills their stockings on Christmas morning, we must eventually come to know that it is God, not Santa Claus, who filled our stockings with legs. "We thank people for birthday presents of cigars and slippers. Can I thank no one for the birthday present of birth?" We can. He has drawn near to Bethlehem to be in reach of our gratitude.

SPRING FASHIONS

have lived almost all my life in a place of seasons, and they have been severe seasons. It has not been possible to miss the passing from winter to spring, or from fall to winter, because the change is so stark. I can't imagine how the passing of a season is even noticed in Hawaii, when it's a matter of going from a balmy 88 degrees to a clement 80 degrees; I grew up accustomed to a Minnesota plunge from a sticky 95 degrees to a frigid -40 (that's true forty below zero; real Minnesotans don't count wind chill).

As I write these words, I live in the more moderated temperatures of Indiana, but I remember noticing spring's arrival this year by an annual rite: the discarding of the winter coat. It brought back memories of how anxiously I awaited the day when I was a child. One day I was sealed in my ponderous, bulky, over-weighted coat, and the next I was free of it. Like Superman ripping apart his Clark Kent shirt and tie on the way to the telephone booth, I zipped apart my jacket and threw it into the house behind me. Spring had come. I was loose again. I had been fettered in the confines of a coat for a season, but now I was set free.

It provoked in me the odd thought of wondering what it would be like if other animals in God's Kingdom followed suit (no pun intended). Spring comes, and the turtle yawns, stretches, then feels for the zipper under his chin and after one smooth pull steps out of his shell. Or perhaps he reaches up behind his neck and pulls his shell over his head like a T-shirt. Unencumbered, he dashes through the grass as speedily as a turtle is able to dash unencumbered. Spring comes, and the snake slithers out of his pants, carelessly leaving them behind in the grass, like a boy strewing his clothes across the bedroom floor.

Spring comes, and the horses kick off their heavy hoofs to run barefoot in the grass, like kids kicking off their galoshes. Spring comes, and the children on the playground doff their snow pants to find they can climb more nimbly; and maybe inside the bulky, lumbering gait of a bear is a lithe and agile creature waiting to step out of its winter woolies.

I have written before of Chesterton's attitude toward clothing. It seems he would have been happier in the clothes Lewis describes in Narnia than the ones he was prescribed to wear in London. Lewis writes, "In Narnia your good clothes were never your uncomfortable ones. They knew how to make things that felt beautiful as well as looking beautiful in Narnia: and there was no such thing as starch or flannel or elastic to be found from one end of the country to the other." Chesterton records a different experience in a letter to Frances. Speaking of himself in third person, he records his dressing ritual:

> He goes through a number of extraordinary and fantastic rituals; which the pompous elfland he has entered demands. The first is that he shall get inside a house of clothing, a tower of wool and flax; that he shall put on this foolish armour solemnly, one piece after another and each in its right place. The things called sleevelinks he attends to minutely. His hair he beats angrily with a bristly tool. For this is the Law.

Clothes make the man, it is often said, and perhaps they make an era, as well. Chesterton often contrasted the drab, grey fashion statement of modernity with the bright-hued medieval fashion. In *The Napoleon of Notting Hill* he describes modern men in frock coats looking like dragons walking backwards, whereas there was once an "ancient sanctity of colours." One of our problems is the lack of both color and sanctity in our clothing. "The modern man thought Becket's robes too rich and his meals too poor. But then the modern man was really exceptional in history; no man before ever ate such elaborate dinners in such ugly clothes."

Clothing—and re-clothing—is a Christian image of the resurrection, described so well by Paul Claudel's meditations on Resurrection from the Dead. "This flick of the nail which will split our pod from top to bottom. . . . Our material body yellows and withers until the seed of immortality is ready." It was not made to last forever in its present form. "This body which we have inherited through a series of intersecting accidents is now rightfully ours through grace," but one day it will be glorified. "The soul therefore surrenders her old tunic to the elements while waiting to be reclothed in that new and innocent garment which He has promised." Our heavenly garments will be white, like light. They will be light. "This is the stuff of our baptismal gown. . . . This is the cloth which heaven supplies to the wardrobe of the Holy Father. This is the linen closet where we would like to plunge our arms and draw forth those noble fabrics with which we would clothe ourselves in folds of glory!"

This will be the Great Spring, when we will slough off our mortality. This will be the Final Spring, when we will find spiritual agility hidden underneath our garments of clay.

SURPRISES

The day is coming, or has just recently passed, when parents around this land will engage in a springtime ritual: the hiding of Easter candy. By the calendar that measures the rise and fall of empires, it was not so very long time ago that my wife and I suffered this awesome responsibility. But by the calendar that measures the speed at which children grow, it seems like a very long time ago, indeed, and makes me nostalgic.

Clearly there are some rules to follow, hard-learned by trial and error. My own father once hid some jelly beans in such an obscure place (behind volume X-Y-Z of the encyclopedias) that we didn't find them until the next October when one of us had a school report to do on yaks. Rule one: hide the jelly beans sufficiently well that they are not immediately seen, but not so well that they are never found. Rule two: hide not with the dust bunnies under the bed. Rule three: from year to year change the hiding places slightly so as to preserve the element of surprise. The hunter should stumble across the treasure, not walk knowingly and deliberately to the piano for black jelly beans on the black keys. Rule four: hide not inside the oven, lest the malted milk balls not be discovered before the preheat is turned on. Rule five: the Easter Bunny must always intend an equal number of treats for each child, for though the Bunny is surprising, he is also fair. Rule six: eggs that were carefully dyed the weekend before should be secreted in the room assigned to each child for search. Rule seven: should a bag be found in the pantry with contents very much like those mounting in the collector's basket, it is a mysterious phenomenon about the existence of Easter Bunny. And the bag is off limits; it should be left untouched.

Wherein lies the captivation of hidden treats? I think it is in the double-take that it causes. Something shows up that doesn't belong. Candy has been misfiled. The keepers of order in the universe must have dozed off, and mischief is afoot. Who knows what else might happen! Everything looks normal to the casual eye—the table and lamp and plant are in their usual place—but something looks different to the careful eye, and requires a second look to register what. I don't remember a five inch chocolate rabbit there yesterday.

Some theorists say that the essence of humor is surprise juxtaposition, that is, the placing of two things together that don't usually belong together, like pants on a mouse. If so, a marshmallow Peep behind the primrose is funny. At least it is fun. It is also evidence. Something happened here before we came on the scene. The trail of candy is like a trail of tracks left by someone who has been at work while we were unaware. The evidence is as real as the tracks of a real rabbit in the mud outside. And since the gift is so delightful, so desirable, so delectable, maybe the giver had us exactly in mind. Maybe he even pictured our face when we stumbled across the secret pleasure. Maybe he is chuckling somewhere now. What we found is so delightful to us, could it have been left by accident?

I think I have just described how Chesterton walked through every day of his life. Every one of his days was filled with double-takes. It was funny, and it was fun. Look at this hansom cab, a chariot for his convenience, and the strange four-legged creature pulling it. Had it been here yesterday? It must have been put here just for his convenience. "How can we contrive to be at once astonished at the world and yet at home in it? How can this queer cosmic town, with its many-legged citizens, with its monstrous and ancient lamps, how can this world give us at once the fascination of a strange town and the comfort and honour of being our own town?" Is it any less hilarious to find a Peep behind a primrose than to find a friend behind every door? "Once I found a friend," Chesterton wrote, and he was surprised the friend was made just for him; "but now I find more and more friends who seem to have been made for me." He thought keeping to one woman a small price for so much as seeing one woman. Who had placed a whole other half of humanity on earth for him to discover when he least expected it? If the cosmos is run by a mysterious power, it is nevertheless a good-natured power, and considering how well everything suits us, it would seem a safe wager that it is run by a power who wishes us well, and has not left it by accident. Perhaps the deity even pictures our faces when we stumble across a pleasure.

Being capable of doing a double-take on reality is a religious attitude. The familiar is sprinkled with surprises, the recognizable is strewn with the fantastic.

The person who is capable of seeing might even be surprised by God peeking out from an unpretentious corner of the world, hidden amongst a guild of carpenters going about their daily work. The same God who plays peek-a-boo from the tomb. Now you see him, now you don't.

A SHRINE OUT OF TIME

I took what seemed to be a step out of time last week, but in a jumbled sort of way, like a dream produces when it gathers images from disjointed places and times. It seemed I was in an Italian hill town in the Middle Ages, for I saw a pilgrimage winding up through a green, wooded hillside to a Romanesque dome and a bell tower jutting out of the forest. It was a shrine to Our Lady and this was the day of its dedication. Leading the procession were acolytes carrying torches and a processional cross before a relic container carried upon the shoulders of four. There were Knights and Ladies of the Holy Sepulchre, a twelfth-century order, in their beret hats and shimmering black capes. Color was added by Knights of Columbus in feathery regalia. I counted about twenty bishops; color was added to their ranks by two cardinals in red. The shrine's walls were fieldstone and limestone blocks, and a burnt orange slate roof below a copper dome. Inside was marble and gold, capital ornamentation, and stained-glass windows that depicted the life of the Blessed Mother.

Then it was as if I was transported to a different place and time. On the wall behind the altar, in its honored place, was a painting of Our Lady of Guadalupe who appeared to St. Juan Diego in 1531. In the courtyard outside the main door of the shrine was a bronze statue of Xocoyte, as the Blessed Mother called Diego when she spoke to him in his native tongue at the apparition. It depicted the moment when he showed Bishop Juan de Zumárraga his cloak upon which an icon of Our Lady of Guadalupe had been miraculously impressed, and from which cascaded roses in December. The relics that were being translated were those of Blessed Miguel Pro, a native of Guadalupe, a Jesuit priest who was executed by a Mexican firing squad in 1927.

And I, myself, arrived at the Pilgrim Center on a large yellow school bus from the shrine's overflow parking lot C. We were just south of LaCrosse, Wisconsin (google "Guadalupe shrine"), yet criss-crossing before my eyes was twelfth-century Italy, fifteenth-century Mexico, and my own American century; gathered together were princes of the Church and lay pilgrims, Hispanics and whites, men and women. And I thought of only one person who could bring these spaces, times, and cultures together like that. Our Lady had summoned the tryst.

Chesterton writes of the difficulty some believers have with Mary, and the even greater difficulty any believer has without Mary. "When I was a boy a more Puritan generation objected to a statue upon my parish church representing the Virgin and Child. After much controversy, they compromised by taking away the Child." He found this odd, as if to wonder how that would satisfy those who worried about Mariolatry. But the attempt turned out to be a parable, he says. "You cannot chip away the statue of a mother from all round that of a new-born child. You cannot suspend the new-born child in mid-air; indeed you cannot really have a statue of a new-born child at all. Similarly, you cannot suspend the idea of a new-born child in the void or think of him without thinking of his mother. You cannot visit the child without visiting the mother." (And so various shrines for visiting are put up, even in the woods of Wisconsin.) "We must admit, if only as we admit it in an old picture, that those holy heads are too near together for the haloes not to mingle and cross."

Some members of that Puritan generation were also present in the dreamy landscape I have been describing. Our bus from parking lot C had to drive past a small group of protestors—I cannot think of another word for the group standing at the entrance to the parking lot holding signs of warning and complaint. I could not make out the smaller print of signs decrying the Rosary, with quotations from the very book from which the Rosary comes. Or the scattered Bible verses that would strip Christ out of the communion of saints, as Chesterton's neighbors chipped Christ out of the arms of his mother. Why is there more honor in isolating Christ than finding him at the head of his body? But one placard was writ large enough for me to catch despite my startled mind. It read, "This is a pagan goddess."

I should have dismounted the bus and asked the carrier whether he meant Mary herself, or whether he meant the Lady of Guadalupe. I should have enlisted the aid of the ACLU in politically, correctly pointing out that the latter maligns the indigenous citizens of South America. I suspect it would have been easier to rally support for Hispanic culture than for Catholic culture, but neither of them think Mary is a goddess. I should have, as Evan MacIan did to Mr. Turnbull in *The Ball and the Cross*, challenged someone to a duel for insulting the honor of Our Lady. But, as both MacIan and Turnbull discovered, this is frowned upon in a society that does not care what you believe so long as you believe it fiercely and privately. Besides, a dreamy and preoccupied state had been cast upon me by my time travel, and I was anxious to begin my ascent up that holy Wisconsin hill.

DUNCAN'S DOCTRINE

Thirteen years ago, when we moved into our present home out of an apartment that did not allow pets, we played the part of good parents and got our children a dog so they could have a taste of nature, even if we weren't going to live the full bucolic life. A six pound peekapoo (pekingese and poodle) seemed quite sufficient to introduce our children to the animal kingdom. Our mutt, Duncan, has fulfilled his purpose admirably well, and has been the occasion of a lot of cuddling, too. He has also been the occasion of a lot of reflection on my part, as I am one never to let a philosophical opportunity go by. The other day afforded such an opportunity when something happened that revealed a capacity that people have and Duncan lacks.

The revelation was occasioned by our having inadvertently left the door to the pantry open, wherein are stored Duncan's liver snacks. Encouraging the small opening at the top of the bag, he downed its entire contents (in a manner fittingly described by reference to his canine lineage: he wolfed it down!) whereupon he promptly went and threw up on the bed. The question this occasioned in my mind was whether my dog had enjoyed a feast? If feasting is measured by no more stringent criterion than how much one can ingest before loosening one's belt at the table, then in that loose manner, I suppose, yes, Duncan had feasted. But the criteria for human feasts usually include thoughtful preparation, family or companionship, and an occasion for the gathering that qualifies it as a celebration. Feasting is a human act that depends upon and derives from human capacities.

Since feasting is constitutive of religious activity, I ventured further in my exercise to suppose Duncan cannot commit religion: he cannot receive sacred ablutions, or light a votive candle, or solicit the heavens by a burnt offering, or fast the forty days up to a holy day, or even know the day is holy. Religiosity is a uniquely human capacity, or so Chesterton would conclude from observing my dog. Religion is a uniquely human product, or so Chesterton did conclude from watching other dogs. "While it is true that a dog has dreams, while most other quadrupeds do not seem even to have that, we have waited a long time for the dog to develop his dreams into an elaborate system or religious ceremonial."

The raw material for religion has lain before the animal kingdom in an accessible and obvious manner for centuries, but "the power of religion was in the mind . . . [and] there is not the faintest hint to suggest that anything short of the human mind we know feels any of these mystical associations at all. A cow in a field seems to derive no lyrical impulse or instruction from her unrivalled opportunities for listening to the skylark. And similarly there is no reason to suppose that live sheep will ever begin to use dead sheep as the basis of a system of elaborate ancestor-worship." They do not schedule feasts, and the obverse is also true. In the same way that I can feast but Duncan can only eat a lot, I can fast but Duncan can only go hungry. Fasting and penitence and hope are uniquely human capacities. "It is not impossible, in the sense of self-contradictory, that we should see cows fasting from grass every Friday or going on their knees as in the old legend about Christmas Eve. It is not in that sense impossible that cows should contemplate death until they can lift up a sublime psalm of lamentation. . . . It is not in that sense impossible that they should express their hopes of a heavenly career in a symbolic dance, in honour of the cow that jumped over the moon."

All this makes me suspect that the so-called nature religions are really not all that natural after all. It is popular sentiment to argue against dogma, ritual, or hierarchy in favor of the religious experience of letting nature's energy flow unimpeded by human institutions, but Chesterton would lead me to conclude that religion does not just lie there in a grassy field to be picked up. The cow experiences nature, too, but "it is obvious that for some reason or other these natural experiences, even natural excitements, never do pass the line that separates them from creative expression like art and religion, in any creature except man." Religiosity is not a passive thing, like catching a cold, but an exceedingly active thing, like constructing a city. And as a *polis* needs politics, religion needs thought. Religion is a great and glorious human construction, one of the things that sets man apart from the animals, but as a human construction it can sometimes go wrong, and has sometimes gone wrong, and will benefit from being more thoughtful, in a human sort of way, not from being more natural, in a bovine sort of way.

The full bag of liver snaps was as inexplicable to Duncan as my existence is inexplicable to me, but he has not been led to either thank the heavens for his gift or curse the heavens for not being beneficent more often. Human beings, however, are faced with the task of interpreting their natural experience of being: does the gift come from a loving God or a trickster?

FANATICAL FASTERS

I am interested in Chesterton as a Catholic. I mean this in both senses the grammar will allow, namely, I am interested inasmuch as he was a Catholic, and inasmuch as I am one too. I realize this is not the only side of the man, and I realize it is not a side that interests everyone, so I don't write about it all the time. But to give a well-rounded glimpse into this well-rounded man, I should be permitted to write about it occasionally.

My stimulus is the tone of a newspaper article. I've forgotten what the article was about and remember better the tone in which it was written: I have forgotten the tune but remember the tenor. The columnist was trying to berate someone and did so by painting him as a rabid Catholic fundamentalist. Whether the subject of this vitriol was deserving, I do not know. Perhaps the person was indeed untrustworthy and could be suspected of performing animal sacrifices in his backyard barbecue pit. I do not know. What interests me is one of the character traits the columnist pointed to as evidence for his Catholic fanaticism: he fasted on Fridays. I find this interesting because I will admit, in a moment of candor, that I also fast on Fridays, although I do not think of myself as a threat to my neighbors.

A leap was being made from an ascetical practice to a person's character. The hard-bitten newspaper man did not know any other people who fasted, and the one man he discovered who did fast was a Catholic, so he took it as typical of Catholic fanaticism. Chesterton also observed how this can happen. Austerity and renunciation "happen to be rare in the modern industrial society of the West. . . . Because it is uncommon for an alderman to fast forty days, or a politician to take a Trappist vow of silence, or a man about town to live a life of strict celibacy, the average outsider is convinced, not only that Catholicism is nothing except asceticism but that asceticism is nothing but pessimism." Say it with me in hushed horror: he fasts on Fridays. The secular journalist is scandalized at the thought of denying oneself anything one wants, any time one wants it, so this must be fanaticism.

Fasting was taken more positively in the Christian ascetical tradition. I take my example from a spiritual guide called *The Ladder of Divine Ascent* by John Climacus (John of the Ladder). "Fasting makes for purity of prayer, an enlightened soul, a watchful mind, a deliverance from blindness. Fasting is the door of compunction, humble sighing, joyful contrition, and end to chatter, an occasion for silence, a custodian of obedience, a lightening of sleep, health of the body, an agent of dispassion, a remission of sins, the gate, indeed the delight of paradise."

But I digress. This is not a column about fasting, it is a column about being aghast at the thought of fasting. More correctly, it is a column about being confused about the command to fast. For the Catholic, fasting fits into the whole. It is a discipline, not a belief. It is a means, not an end. Therefore the faster knows how to weigh its importance. And that is what the non-Catholic journalist did not understand.

Chesterton recognized the same tenor about a different tune in a piece written in his day. The writer of that piece seemed to take Rome as

> a powerful and persecuting superstition, intoxicated with the impious idea of having a monopoly of divine truth, and therefore cruelly crushing and exterminating everything else as error. It burns thinkers for thinking, discoverers for discovering, philosophers and theologians who differ by a hair's breadth from its dogmas; it will tolerate no tiny change or shadow of variety even among its friends and followers; it sweeps the whole world with one encyclical cyclone of uniformity; it would destroy nations and empires for a word, so wedded is it to its fixed idea that its own word is the Word of God.

With such a picture of Rome Chesterton could understand how the writer was puzzled why eastern-rite Catholic priests (called Uniates in Chesterton's day) were allowed to grow beards while Latin priests were required to be clean-shaven. Inexplicable!

When [Rome] is thus sweeping the world, it comes to a remote and rather barbarous region somewhere on the borders of Russia; where it stops suddenly; smiles broadly; and tells the people there that they can have the strangest heresies they like. . . . We might well suppose, therefore, that the Church says benevolently to these fortunate Slavs, "By all means worship Baphomet and Beelzebub; say the Lord's Prayer backwards; continue to drink the blood of infants—nay, even," and here her voice falters, till she rallies with an effort of generous resolution, "—yes, even, if you really must, grow a beard."

How can Chesterton begin to explain the place of authority, the hierarchy of truths, the fact "that a married clergy is a matter of discipline and not doctrine, that it can therefore be allowed locally without heresy—when all the time the man thinks a beard is as important as a wife and more important than a false religion?"

And how can I explain that obedience in the matter of fasting is not fanaticism in other matters of thought?

A DO-IT-YOURSELF ESSAY

Presented for your afternoon's entertainment is a "do-it-yourself" *Gilbert* essay, to be constructed as you would a swing set in the backyard, or a bookshelf in the den. It comes with the sort of instructions that say "insert tab C into slot B," or "use Phillips head and half inch screw on board X."

Recently an article appeared in *Time Magazine* that was struggling to make up its mind whether it would be a news report or a weak editorial. The news that it was trying to report is that the English translation of the third revised Roman missal will appear in November 2011. But the reporter appears to have let a wee bit of personal bias creep into his opening sentence. "Back in Christianity's early days, petty semantics could cause powerful schisms. . . . But if you thought modern Christendom was beyond that kind of medieval nonsense, think again." Having been informed that the article will be about petty semantic nonsense, the reader is further warned that this time the foolishness is not merely academic. "It's tempting to dismiss the clash with the old saying about fights inside academia: they're so fierce because the stakes are so low. But the Catholic missal melee is unfortunately a reminder that the tiresome practice of theological hairsplitting is still alive and well in the 21st century." Although we might tolerate such conversation for academics, the world will disapprove it here. "Either way, we Catholics look a little foolish right now—and not very Christ-like. Jesus was a master of simple but beautiful parables told in simple but beautiful language: he knew better than to substitute 'incarnate' for 'born.' And he knew there are better things to fight for than petty semantics."

Now, gentle reader, I will spill out the rest of the boards and bolts you will need for your construction. Has Chesterton ever commented on the themes tiresomely reemerging in this article? Yes. And your construction task is to decide which Chesterton tabs you will choose to insert into the holes contained in this argument.

Tab A. Chesterton reports reading in his London newspaper a plea from a woman to make Christianity more simple. It is a refrain frequently heard: all that Jesus, the parable spinner on the shores of Galilee, meant to say was a simple message of love and brotherhood, so why have we cumbered our religion with long technical words and senseless ceremonies? Chesterton's reply to her is that "you cannot make a success of anything, even loving, entirely without thinking." He imagines her plea in the spiritual realm being made in the medical realm, and suggests it would sound like saying "All I ask is Health; what could be simpler than the beautiful gift of Health? Why not be content to enjoy for ever the glow of youth and the fresh enjoyment of being fit?"

But thinking about complicated things is sometimes required for simple health. It is like she is asking,

> Why study dry and dismal sciences of anatomy and physiology; why inquire about the whereabouts of obscure organs in the human body? Why pedantically distinguish between what is labelled a poison and what is labelled an antidote, when it is so simple to enjoy Health? Of course health is preferable to disease, but the restoration of health requires some careful attention. We cannot say, Why worry with a minute exactitude about the number of drops of laudanum or the strength of a dose of chloral, when it is so nice to be healthy? Away with your priestly apparatus of stethoscopes and clinical thermometers; with your ritualistic mummery of feeling pulses, putting out tongues, examining teeth, and the rest!

In fact, Chesterton concludes, "if Christ had remained on earth for an indefinite time, trying to induce men to love one another, He would have found it necessary to have some tests, some methods, some way of dividing true love from false love, some way of distinguishing between tendencies that would ruin love and tendencies that would restore it."

Tab B. Chesterton defined theology as "that part of religion that requires brains." And why would one need theology in addition to religion? To gauge, judge, protect, and direct religious enthusiasms.

It is exactly this which explains the monstrous wars about small points of theology, the earthquakes of emotion about a gesture or word. It is only a matter of an inch; but an inch is everything when you are balancing. . . . Once let one idea become less powerful and some other idea would become too powerful. . . . The idea of birth through a Holy Spirit, of the death of a divine being, of the forgiveness of sins, or the fulfillment of prophecies, are ideas which, any one can see, need but a touch to turn them into something blasphemous or ferocious.

Tab C. Why has the church put all her resources to this task? Petty semantics? Or does human happiness depend upon understanding our relationship with Almighty God adequately, and expressing it correctly? "If some small mistake were made in doctrine, huge blunders might be made in human happiness. A sentence phrased wrong about the nature of symbolism would have broken all the best statues in Europe. A slip in the definitions might stop all the dances; might wither all the Christmas trees or break all the Easter eggs."

I leave you, now, to construct Chesterton's response yourself.

HOPE FOR POTTERHEADS

I have always been in the position of an eavesdropper when it comes to Harry Potter, and my status has not changed since the last, and only other, time I wrote about the phenomenon. Were our children younger, I'm sure I would be better versed from an evening exercise at bedtime, but without children to pull me into Hogwarts, I don't know if I shall ever go there on my own accord.

But only a hermit, or someone obstinate on principle, could have avoided the hubbub over the appearance of the final book. Since I am neither a hermit, nor someone obstinately opposed to Harry Potter on principle, I took note of this hubbub. Was one of the characters going to die in the last installment? That was the paramount question in people's curiosity, placed there by Ms. Rowling herself in a well-timed interview some months before where she admitted that a major character would, indeed, die. (My eavesdropping also notes that she has created a more recent sensation, with another more recent interview concerning Dumbledore, but I am not commenting on that here. I am only thinking about the clamor that surrounded the appearance of the final volume in the series.) We all know now how it turns out. The worst fears of Potterheads was realized, after all. Harry does die. But Harry also comes back. He stands up again. I pause to note that the Greek word for resurrection, written atop the icons, is *anastasis,* from *ana,* again, and *stasis,* to stand.

What I am interested in observing right now is something about ourselves. When Ms. Rowling said one of the major characters would die, this option did not forcefully dawn on anyone's mind. It was as if a great trick was played on millions of Potterheads, with no one guessing any other ending to a story that would end with a death.

That is worth noticing at this time of year, in the Christmas season, which is the beginning of a story which eventually ends with the death of its major character, too, but a story in which that is not the final ending, either. At Christmas begins the story of a man whose story contains a plot twist that rescues Potterheads from bitter disappointment. How interesting that no one thought of it! Is that a comment about how washed out the Christian story of the resurrection has become? The story is in our memories, but faded—like the print of an old newspaper which has been faded by the years, and become brittle, and is so washed out that it is not potent enough to break through the air of rationalism by which we read our newspapers and even our fantasies.

Perhaps we need a shock, a jolt, more powerful than could come from a wand bought at Olivanders. Chesterton wrote, "I suggested recently that people would see the Christian story if it could only be told as a heathen story. The Faith is simply the story of a God who died for men. But, queerly enough, if we were even to print the words without a capital G, as if it were the cult of some new and nameless tribe, many would realize the idea for the first time. Many would feel the thrill of a new fear and sympathy if we simply wrote 'the story of a god who died for men.' People would sit up suddenly and say what a beautiful and touching pagan religion that must be." What a beautiful and touching story it must be to have a student wizard die for his friends.

I know this risks confusing reality with fantasy, the Gospel with magic, truth with stories, but it is just possible that the real Gospel truth can bore its way into our minds through fantastic and magical stories.

When C. S. Lewis talks about the Eucharist, he knows the truth of transubstantiation, but he can describe it in other terms. "Here is big medicine and strong magic. When I say 'magic' I am not thinking of the paltry and pathetic techniques by which fools attempt and quacks pretend to control nature. I mean rather what is suggested by fairy-tale sentences like 'This is a magic flower and if you carry it the seven gates will open to you of their own accord,' or 'This is a magic cave and those who enter it will renew their youth.' I should define magic in this sense as 'objective efficacy which cannot be further analyzed.'"

Is Potter fantasy? Of course. But that a person might hope to "stand up again from the dead" is a hope written deep into our natures. When Mr. Blatchford sought to discredit Christianity by pointing out that the Christian plot line is to be found in pagan myths (and, we can now add, in children's literature), Chesterton replied "If the Christian God really made the human race, would not the human race tend to rumours and perversions of the Christian God? . . . If we were so made that a Son of God must deliver us, is it odd that Patagonians should dream of a Son of God?" And if we were so made to share the ending of the man whose story begins at Christmas, and join him at the right hand of his Father, raised from the death, is it odd that such an ending would be so satisfying to Potterheads?

STONED

I can't exactly recall in what movie I've seen this, because I think I've seen it in several movies. An intrepid explorer has found a key which is a stone that fits into a hollow. The key was overlooked by others because it looked ordinary, like all the other stones; or perhaps the key was inherited from a father and held by our hero without suspicion about its capacity. The key is precious, and probably the hero has been defending it for half the movie from thieves, because when this key is finally inserted and turned, the most amazing effects result. Secret panels slide open, a portion of a wall revolves to reveal a treasure room, the gate to Atlantis opens, the blocks of a pyramid shift and rearrange themselves into an ascending stair case. By turning this one stone, all the other stones move. By magic, the stones float in mid-air until they settle into their proper places.

This scene is not so much a particular memory as a feeling, and I had occasion to remember the feeling on a recent trip. Squeezed into the summer schedule between obligations, my wife and I took ten days in Paris. And on our first day of that vacation (or the second, depending how you count the day of arrival and late afternoon jetlag sleep), we took the Metro to the Cathedral of Notre Dame. We had been there before, but those times on a more rushed itinerary that allowed us only three days to do all of Paris before catching the Eurail to another city. So on that first visit we had done Notre Dame, the Louvre, Museum D'Orsay, Eiffel Tower, Seine boat ride, L'Arc de Triomphe, Rodin museum, Champs-Elysées, and a baguette and cheese sandwich in the Luxembourg Gardens all in seventy-two hours. On this second visit, traveling alone and without consideration of the children's attention span, we took as much time as we wanted at Notre Dame.

After a few hours of walking, and listening to an audio self-guided tour, and lighting a candle at a chapel, and looking at the sacristy museum, we sat down. We just sat and absorbed the atmosphere of the place. And I began watching other tourists. They were now, like I had just been doing, craning their necks to follow the graceful arch line to the ceiling. They were looking at these stones piled one atop another in the Gothic fashion; at the stone that had been carved into a statue of an angel or king of Israel; outside there had been stones flying up into buttresses to steady the groaning of the wall's weight. How had these stones been hoisted so high?

At that moment a bell struck. Not a clock bell, but a church bell, for Notre Dame has a noon mass. And as it would be impractical to close the cathedral daily and shoo the tourists out, like ducklings out of the pond, the people who wanted to pray went to a roped off area in the middle of the nave, and the people who wanted to tour continued their slow migration around the nave behind the ropes. From there they continued to look. From there they continued to take pictures. Some took photographs of what was to them a very foreign-looking rite, and camera lenses clicked as the white-robed concelebrants processed up to the altar. A stone altar! A *Lapis Iste*—the stone table of Abel and Solomon, foreshadowing Christ who is the rock of salvation.

And then I thought: this is the key! This is the stone that moved all the other stones into their places. The other stones have piled themselves one atop another to honor this stone, perhaps floating at the end of a medieval pulley. It was in tribute to this one stone that the others have arranged themselves. This stone is the reason for Notre Dame. It is the reason why these blocks have migrated to this place from their quarry pit. The priest says a word that moves heaven's storehouse, and stones stand up in praise; by the motion the priest makes over this stone, all the other stones move into place.

Beyond the walls of this building other stones were compiled (*com+pila* means a heap of stones): the city of Paris, the cities of France, the cities of Europe. They were taken from the crumbled stones of the Roman Empire (*compilare* means to plunder). The Roman Empire had fallen, and the circuses and coliseums that had once spilled blood in sport were now dilapidated ruins (*dis+lapidâre* means undone stones). Peter, no stranger to rocks himself, took the building blocks of Rome and stacked them up around a new ideal. Chesterton and Belloc were agreed that Christianity is the reason for Europe, and Europe is the product of Christianity. Around the keystone of Golgotha's stone, a civilization suddenly stood up in salute.

Today we live off the capital, but the social sanities that we take for granted won't remain upright without their keystone. They require a theological creed as a grounding principle. Chesterton writes, "All such social sanities are now the traditions of old Catholic dogmas. Like many other Catholic dogmas, they are felt in some vague way even by heathens, so long as they are healthy heathens."

INTELLIGIBILITY

I was in school for a very long time; you may just ask my longsuffering wife. And as a result, I have written lots, and lots of papers of nearly every stripe and variety: research papers, editorial papers, argumentative papers, historical-critical papers. Therefore, when my son asked whether I would be willing and able to look over one of his papers, I optimistically agreed, being willing and thinking I was able.

He is in a master's program in music performance, and was required to write a paper on Gustav Mahler, and it was filled with sentences such as these:

- The large chords in the brass measures 119 and 123 interrupt the flow of the woodwind theme. The B flat to E flat seems to suggest a V-I cadence in E flat which is the neapolitan of D major.
- The melodic shape has a small range, staying within a fifth for the most part, but the motion is kept going by the dotted half notes, syncopations, and tied notes, always creating a sense of arsis through the upbeats.
- Bar 783 has a return of the brass playing the unison B flat disrupting the D major tonality.

A friend of mine was asked to review a particularly hard book, and confided to me that when he agreed he was thinking, "It's in English. What could be so difficult?" I knew how he felt reading my son's paper.

A sentence might be unintelligible for a variety of reasons. Or, said another way, its intelligibility must be built upon a series of compounding steps from alphabet to word to syntax to language to content.

First, the letters must be from an alphabet that one knows (if we had the font available, I would put a sentence in Greek here). Second and third, there must be a correct order inside the word ("gifrafe") and between the words ("cat away tree ran dog from up"). This is spelling and syntax. It's interesting that you can run a spell check on words, but not on a column of numbers. The sequence of the digits inside the number *is* the meaning, but the sequence of letters inside the word is only a step to the meaning of the sentence. That's why there could even be meaning with inaccurate spelling, as this example from the internet shows, with apologies to this issue's proof checker: "Eye halve a spelling checker. It came width my pea see. It plainly marques four my revue Miss steaks eye kin knot sea." Fourth, one must know the language. "Kommst du morgen Abendzuunserer Party?" is unintelligible if one does not speak German. "f(x) = 3x − 10" is unintelligible if one does not speak algebra. They are both languages. And fifth, the content must make sense. I struggled with Alfred North Whitehead when he wrote "An actual entity is to be conceived both a subject presiding over its own immediacy of becoming, and a superject which is the atomic creature exercising its function of objective immortality."

Chesterton spoke about theology being a language he had to learn when he became a Catholic. "I might remark that much of it consists of the act of translation; of discovering the real meaning of words, which the Church uses rightly and the world uses wrongly. For instance, the convert discovers that 'scandal' does not mean 'gossip'; . . . Scandal means scandal, what it originally meant in Greek and Latin: the tripping up of somebody else when he is trying to be good." So as there are specialists in math and Mahler, in German and philosophy and German philosophy, there might be specialists in theology who know the meaning of a foreign term, an abbreviated term, a specialized term, or a term that has accrued meaning as it rolled through history. No other word but "transubstantiation" will do; it's best not to use "consubstantiation."

But even though one does not speak the specialized language, f(x) = 3x − 10 is still true, and I might be taught to better appreciate Mahler even without realizing that the melodic shape stayed within a fifth. In other words, being able to *explain* something with specialized jargon, isn't the same as appreciating the thing explained. Michael Polanyi says, "We know more than we can say." And the things we want to appreciate are truth, goodness, and beauty. As one of my teachers observed, why is it that being smarter doesn't mean you're necessarily more virtuous? He went on to speak about having a "grammar of life." Not only our letters within the word, but also our actions within our life should follow a certain shape, or order. When thought is ordered it is logical; when a life is ordered it is virtuous.

Chesterton liked to infuse creative innovation inside logic (like depending on fairy tales to crack open the rational mind), but about the order of virtue he was adamant. "I am ordinary in the correct sense of the term; which means the acceptance of an order; a Creator and the Creation, the common sense of gratitude for Creation, life and love as gifts permanently good, marriage and chivalry as laws rightly controlling them, and the rest of the normal traditions of our race and religion." Only in such a way can a life become intelligible, to ourselves, to others, and most of all to God when we must give account of our life.

PART 5
Transcendent Truths

"It would be impossible to pay a more complete tribute to the truth of a philosophy than to say that nobody understands it except a few people who have found it to be true."
March 8, 1924

A WAR OF THE WORDS

've never been much good at fiction, or at children's literature, so my odds at success with children's fiction are pretty slim. But suppose I were to suffer a kind of mid-life crisis career change, and turn from writing about theology to writing tales for children. I might begin with something like this:

"The elf and goblin made their way through a holly covered entrance between the ash and willow trees. The magpie and canary brought marzipan and cauliflower, and there was liquorice, too. Nearby, in the abbey, the bishop christened a sinner that Pentecost, and the saints rejoiced. And at the castle, where monarchs ruled the land, the coronation of a duchess and duke was celebrated in the empire."

As eager as I am, myself, to see where this tale might go, and how these three sets of characters might interact a few pages further on, I pause to make my point.

If you were a child in England, around or past the age of seven, and were you ignorant of one of the nouns in my opening lines, you would no longer be able to turn for help to the children's dictionary from Oxford Press, for my sentences are constructed entirely with words that have been *removed* from the most recently published edition.

When defense was made for striking these words, the head of children's dictionaries pointed out that "We are limited by how big the dictionary can be— little hands must be able to handle it." No mention was made that little heads must also be able to handle fairy tales. Offering further apologetic, the head of children's dictionaries noted that once upon a time (a phrase whose fate in the dictionary I have not yet learned) dictionaries for children had lots of examples of flowers, because "many children lived in semi-rural environments and saw the seasons. Nowadays, the environment has changed." Making application of the argument, she observed the change in our environment, and the effect it has had upon the dictionary's content. "We are also much more multicultural. People don't go to church as often as before. Our understanding of religion is within multiculturalism, which is why some words such as 'Pentecost' or 'Whitsun' would have been in twenty years ago but not now."

So how would I have to rewrite my opening paragraph, using only words that have been *added* in the new edition? Perhaps something like this: "The celebrity was tolerant of boisterous and alliterated blogs, and never cut and pasted debates into his chat room. Most colloquial idiom was common sense, but this dyslexic citizen presented a cautionary tale. Such vandalism would endanger the interdependent and democratic apparatus if the database was exported to voicemail."

Ah, yes, that's more like it. A recognizable world, a world filled with things that go clank, and beeps that announce email, and values of toleration touted by celebrities who have not studied. Only, if this is my regular world, why would I need a dictionary to understand it? If I know what the Euro is (a word added), but do not know what an elf is (a word removed), isn't the latter exactly the word for which I need a dictionary? Such is the point made by some of the new dictionary's critics: "The word selections are a very interesting reflection of the way childhood is going, moving away from our spiritual background and the natural world and towards the world that information technology creates for us."

Instead of words creating a world, we have a world created by our words. But who are the creators? And what are they creating?

I believe Chesterton would observe a common feature of the words that make up our daily, technological world. He would say that they are specialized words, and therefore they cannot describe universal things. The ancient and universal things, he would say, are capacious because they are not specialized, and in not being specialized, they have more uses than our modern substitutes for them.

> If a man found a coil of rope in a desert he could at least think of all the things that can be done with a coil of rope; and some of them might even be practical. He could tow a boat or lasso a horse. He could play cat's cradle, or pick oakum. He could construct a rope-ladder for an eloping heiress, or cord her boxes for a traveling maiden aunt. He could learn to tie a bow, or he

could hang himself. Far otherwise with the unfortunate traveler who should find a telephone in the desert. You can telephone with a telephone; you cannot do anything else with it.

The same is true of words. With universal words like "elf, altar, duchess, saint, sin, monastery, psalm, beaver, lark, acorn and parsnip" I could write a universal tale, a tale about universal things, a tale in which every child could imagine himself. But with specialized words like "broadband, MP3 player, attachment, biodegradable, endangered, trapezium, and block graph" I can write about the internet, but I cannot write about anything else with them.

Odd, then, that in the name of being multicultural we have surrendered being universal! By denying the word "monastery" to both the Christian child and the Muslim child we have taken away a universal image of a man or woman who strives for God—something common to them both. And we have left them with metallic-sounding words, that are only shared in common if they are of the same income bracket.

BACKWARD REASONING

Aside benefit to reading Chesterton is learning to argue better, that is, more clearly. One might not think of him as an instructor in logic because he does not dangle the trappings of a professor (I mean, he does not talk about talking; plus, when he talks, he is interesting). But in point of fact, he is a mentor and guide to clear argument because he listened to what people said, and then he would test the assumption behind what they said. I find that this is a rare talent, and I do not say my training is yet complete in this regard, but I have an example of a recent episode in which I listened as Chesterton listened—that is, to the assumption.

There was a round of discussions on my campus surrounding a policy decision by the administration. Because this column should have some universal applicability, I will spare you the particulars and only say that some were in favor of the decision, and others against it. During the course of interactions between these two factions, I heard the following statement made by a disputant: "Let's not go back to an old Catholic morality." I listened expectantly, with baited breath, for the reason why not to go back to an old Catholic morality. Perhaps he knew of some secret reason why the old morality was not Catholic, or why the old Catholic teaching was flawed. Perhaps he had discovered a suppressed line of reasoning that extended from ancient heresies down to the recent past, that stopped miraculously exactly fifty years ago, and that was why he did not want to return to that particular old morality.

Alas, my expectations were dashed. He never said why it was wrong to go back to this old Catholic morality. He seemed to think it self-evidently wrong simply because it consisted of "going back."

That is when Chesterton's attentiveness crept into my consciousness. I asked myself whether going back is always undesirable. For example, a scout troop is out for a wooded hike and stops for a picnic by a stream; and after re-packing their gear they march the children down a path for twenty minutes before they notice that one of the children is missing; but the scout master resolutely announces "We cannot go back for it is the essence of a hike to go forward." For example, you notice that your bank has made a mistake entering a figure, and before you have a chance to bring it to correction, the next six transactions have already been recorded, and the computer has done its addition and subtraction in a tenth of a second, and the wrong figure enters into next month's balance resulting in an overdraft on six more checks. When you beg the clerk to double-check last month's figures, the bank manager resolutely announces, "We cannot go back over past transactions." For example, you are on a drive to California but exit hastily onto ramp A instead of ramp B, and now find yourselves headed toward Maine, but when the wife gently points out the error, the husband says resolutely, and with all the dignity a lost male can muster, "We cannot go back if we want to make any progress."

Obviously, going back is wrong if it takes you in the wrong way. But if you are already going the wrong way, then backtracking *is* a sign of progress. And whether going back to an old Catholic morality is progress is exactly the argument I never heard. I never heard the argument because it was not given, and it was not given because it was thought unnecessary, and it was not thought necessary because everyone in the room assumed that "going back" is always bad.

Chesterton writes that every epoch has its own assumption, and by that assumption the epoch is characterized. He characterizes our epoch's assumption by the term "inevitability." "We are subconsciously dominated in all departments by the notion that there is no turning back, and it is rooted in materialism and the denial of free will." The basic modern sense is this: "that as the future is inevitable, so is the past irrevocable." We have been trained to think this way. So we will reform, but we will not repeal. Chesterton tells of a politician who, "having said, in a heat of temporary sincerity, that he would repeal an Act, actually had to write to all the papers to assure them that he would only amend it."

The modern world thinks by means of the category of evolution the way the ancient world thought by the category of emanation. We unconsciously associate evolution with forward direction. Life moves forward, so to go backward means to become more primitive, less developed, an amoeba instead of a jellyfish. We think to deliberately choose to go backward is devolution, a regression, like preferring the medieval peasant who thought the world was flat. But even if this is true in the world of scientific fact (sometimes it pays for them to go back and check things again, too), it doesn't apply in the world of moral fact, at all. Morality cannot be judged by direction. If there was more truth, and beauty, and goodness in the ideals of a previous age, who would object to returning to recover it?

ADVICE TO NEW PARENTS

There was a philosophy making its appearance already in Chesterton's day that had a plan for the improvement of the human race through a sort of sanitation of the mind. If the body of man could attain greater health through diet and calisthenics, then the psyche of man could attain greater health through a strict regimen of what it is fed, too, and by being exercised upon certain forward ideas. This was not oral hygiene, it was psychic hygiene. And not coincidentally, as it was the poorer classes who suffered from dirt in their homes because they were not paid a working wage to have a leisured home-maker, so also it was the lower class poor who might need some psychological tidying up. The reformer was always ready to tell the lower class how to improve the way they raised their children.

Of the many suggestions handed on unbidden by this busybody, the suggestion that most galled Chesterton was the one objecting to fairy tales. In our own day, this objection comes from the progressive parent who swears that instead of fairy tales they would rather pass the hour scheduled with the toddler showing flash cards of French verbs and photographs of famous faces while Mozart plays in the background. Fairy tales are cotton candy: substanceless spun sugar that will decay the mind like sugary sweets will decay the teeth. If we want our children to have healthy gums, and good posture, and lean builds, then surely we do not want flabby fairy tales floating around in their minds either. In Chesterton's day, the objection came from the protective parent, who objected to fairy tales because they were too frightening. "I find that there really are human beings who think fairy tales bad for children. . . . [A] lady has written me an earnest letter saying that fairy tales ought not to be taught to children even if they are true. She says that it is cruel to tell children fairy tales, because it frightens them. You might just as well say that it is cruel to give girls sentimental novels because it makes them cry."

He mounts his defense. "All this kind of talk is based on that complete forgetting of what a child is like which has been the firm foundation of so many educational schemes." Yes, fairy tales are alarming when witches are baked in ovens, and disobedient girls find a wolf in Grandma's bed, and toes are cut off to fit into shoes (the original ending of Cinderella when the stepsister tries to fit her foot into the glass slipper). This is not a hygienic and salubrious setting for children. But Chesterton's point is that the world is an alarming place, and children already know that before we get there with the big book of the Brothers Grimm to teach them this fact. "If you keep bogies and goblins away from children they would make them up for themselves. One small child in the dark can invent more hells than Swedenborg. One small child can imagine monsters too big and black to get into any picture, and give them names too unearthly and cacophonous to have occurred in the cries of any lunatic. . . . The timidity of the child or the savage is entirely reasonable; they are alarmed at this world, because this world is a very alarming place."

The question now is what to do about it. What shall we do, given that we live in an alarming world? There would be an ultimate irony if the progressive parent were actually in favor of retarding the child's progress in learning to deal with upsetting things. And it would be equally ironic if the protective parent, who wanted above all to increase the child's aptitudes and inherent abilities, would now reverse course and choose to deny the child this early opportunity for learning what to do about fearful things. For that is the lesson Chesterton thinks fairy tales teach.

> Fairy tales, then, are not responsible for producing in children fear, or any of the shapes of fear; fairy tales do not give the child the idea of the evil or the ugly; that is in the child already, because it is in the world already. Fairy tales do not give the child his first idea of bogey. *What fairy tales give the child is his first clear idea of the possible defeat of bogey.* The baby has known the dragon intimately ever since he had an imagination. What the fairy tale provides for him is a St. George to kill the dragon.

Of course, all this advice to new parents might well be misleading if the fairy tales in question are some modern tale with no moral code. Perhaps we are leaning in that direction. Perhaps we have grown jaded by the idea of courage and heroism, and some avant-garde publisher has released a new version—perhaps as a video game—in which the dragon kills St George, just to be different. Then we will have forgotten the purpose of fairy tales, and the new tales might not be worth the breath it takes to read them at bedtime.

CHESTERTON, NATURALLY

It is difficult to imagine Chesterton on a camping trip in the wild, roughing it, paddling his canoe by day and pitching a tent at night to fry up a trout caught in the lake, with the chatter of birds in the treetops overhead. It is easier to imagine Chesterton on a daily trip in the city, taking a hansom cab to settle himself in the pub to eat some fish and chips caught in a lake somewhere nearby, to the accompanying chatter of fellow diners chatting merrily in the booth next door.

It would seem that Chesterton did love nature, but he was not a member of the "love of nature" movement, whose founding principle seemed to be that only nature is good, and that natural means whatever is untouched by man. In other words, Chesterton could appreciate both natural things as they are, and artifacts made by man. On the one hand, he constantly calls us back to appreciate the magic of natural things. "I do not think there is anyone who takes quite such fierce pleasure in things being themselves as I do. The startling wetness of water excites and intoxicates me: the fieriness of fire, the steeliness of steel, the unutterable muddiness of mud." On the other hand, he can equally call us to appreciate the magic of artificial things. "The false type of naturalness harps always on the distinction between the natural and the artificial. The higher kind of naturalness ignores that distinction. To the child the tree and the lamp-post are as natural and as artificial as each other; or rather, neither of them are natural but both supernatural. For both are splendid and unexplained. The flower with which God crowns the one, and the flame with which Sam the lamplighter crowns the other, are equally of the gold of fairy-tales."

I think this accounts for Chesterton's occasional critiques of what I shall call "simplicity movements." "It does not so very much matter whether a man eats a grilled tomato or a plain tomato; it does very much matter whether he eats a plain tomato with a grilled mind." Tangled up with this simple naturalism, which prefers organic tomatoes, was the ideal of the personal and solitary development of our individual natures. "A man approaches, wearing sandals and simple raiment, a raw tomato held firmly in his right hand, and says, 'The affections of family and country alike are hindrances to the fuller development of human love;' but the plain thinker will only answer him, with a wonder not untinged with admiration, 'What a great deal of trouble you must have taken in order to feel like that.'"

These lines came to mind when I was recently made aware of a movement that takes the "back to nature" movement to an extreme which can only stir a wonder not untinged with admiration. I refer to a movement that is rigorously honest in its logic. Nature is good; unnatural is bad; the unnatural is anything that has been touched by the hand of man; therefore, to return to goodness we must not only stop interfering with nature, we must do away with the interferer. They call themselves the Voluntary Human Extinction Movement, or VHEMT for short (pronounced *vehement*, their web page instructs).

As I say, one must admire the consistency of their thought even as one wonders at the great deal of trouble they must have taken to feel this way. If unaffected nature is good, and human beings affect nature, then only "phasing out the human race by voluntarily ceasing to breed will allow Earth's biosphere to return to good health"—the health of the biosphere being preferred to ours. If human beings disrupt natural cycles, then do away with the disruptions by doing away with the disrupters.

In a nod of altruism, VHEMT will not force their conclusions on others by violent means, but rather they prefer to encourage people to simply step up to their responsibility and stop procreating. VHEMT volunteers know that "the hopeful alternative to the extinction of millions of species of plants and animals is the voluntary extinction of one species: Homo sapiens. Us. Each time another one of us decides not to add another one of us to the burgeoning billions already squatting on this ravaged planet, another ray of hope shines through the gloom." This is a simple solution. And a natural one. And it is sensible so long as all biological species are equal, and one does possess spirit and free will that makes it exceptional.

The pagan world had seen contentious relationships between man and nature before, Chesterton observed, but Christianity insists on a different relationship. "Nature is not our mother: Nature is our sister. We can be proud of her beauty, since we have the same father; but she has no authority over us; we have to admire, but not to imitate. . . . Nature was a solemn mother to the worshippers of Isis and Cybele. Nature was a solemn mother to Wordsworth or to Emerson. But Nature is not solemn to Francis of Assisi or to George Herbert. To Francis, Nature is a sister, and even a younger sister: a little, dancing sister, to be laughed at as well as loved." Admire Nature, but do not imitate her ways. Not even as concerns extinctions.

A MOST UN-MATERNAL MOTHER

A not uncommon pastime of certain advanced thinkers in the twentieth— excuse me, twenty-first century (I mustn't forget to keep up with our advancements)—is to play "pity the pagan." This game is most easily played in the absence of any real knowledge about ancient pagans. The way it works is to amass your sympathies over some aspect of ancient science or culture or religion. In my circles the most fun is to pity the pagan for the gods he had to endure: fearful and dreadful gods who fixed fates and decreed destinies with iron wills; inexorable and unapproachable gods; supernal gods who stood so far above earth they were incapable of pity for us; relentless gods who crushed individuals beneath the wheel of fate; gods who were themselves powerless to change the laws, and would vouchsafe no petition to do so.

Oh, wait. I'm sorry. I was on the wrong page. I was describing modernity's concept of nature, instead. This is a description of how we understand nature to work. Though it is the pagans we pity for living under a force that is deaf to human desires and blind to human needs, this is, in fact, what we think of nature, even if we soften the harshness by calling her "Mother." But that is a sham. There is nothing maternal about Mother Nature. She will not listen to us, or respond to us, and hardly takes notice of us. She raises up whole species and wipes them out without intent or regret. She places all her hope in the survival of the fittest few, and is willing to sacrifice the redundant remainder. She forfeits the individual so long as the genus thrives. Once set, she does not deviate course, but impersonally pursues her evolutionary course. Since she deals in millennia and eons and ages, the temporary is of no interest to her, except as means to an end. Except she has no end, in the sense of purpose. She made the rabbit to be eaten by the fox, but we don't know why she made the fox. Pity the poor pagan? It is we who live in the colder universe. Their gods may have lived on Mt. Olympus, but at least they were not indifferent to us; we have invented an indifferent goddess.

When Chesterton espoused freedom in man and providence in God he was aware of being out of step with his times, and, as usual, being out of step with his times meant he was a step ahead of our time. The dikes he chose to shore up forecasted whence the threats to our humanity would come. In 1903 Robert Blatchford declared in an article in his newspaper, the *Clarion*, that the case for science was complete. Human fictions such as free will and responsibility could be replaced by social facts, facts such as social environment and social conditioning. Do away with slums by a little social engineering, which seeks to translate Mother Nature's method onto the Socialist State. The fitter rules the weaker, and the parliamentarian legislates the slum dweller. Blatchford's moral improvement consisted of telling people they weren't responsible for anything because everything was a result of environment and heredity. The Socialist state will gladly change the environment, and eugenics will gladly change our heredity.

In reply to Mr. Blatchford, Chesterton argued that he has conceived a person more imprisoned by impersonal forces than our pagan predecessors could have imagined.

> There is a liberty that has made men happy in dungeons, as it may make them happy in slums. It is the liberty of the mind, that is to say, it is the one liberty on which Mr. Blatchford makes war. That which all the tyrants have left, he would extinguish. . . . More numerous than can be counted, in all the wars and persecutions of the world, men have looked out of their little grated windows and said "at least my thoughts are free." "No, No," says the face of Mr. Blatchford, suddenly appearing at the window, "your thoughts are the inevitable result of heredity and environment. Your thoughts are as material as your dungeons. Your thoughts are as mechanical as the guillotine." So pants this strange comforter from cell to cell. . . . Many have admitted Fatalism as a melancholy and metaphysical truth. No one before him, as far as I know, ever took it round with a big drum as a cheery means of moral improvement.

Blatchford would feel vindicated by reading the spate of recent articles in popular magazines that have patiently explained to me how much of me is genetically determined by Mother Nature. The behavior of mothers and fathers is scripted by millions of years of biological necessity, I am told, and one cannot eradicate the violence instilled by ancestors who fought off the hyena for a scrap of food. It would appear I am bound by Mother Nature in Blatchford's dungeon by my DNA chain.

In Christianity, says Chesterton, "Nature is not our mother: Nature is our sister. We can be proud of her beauty, since we have the same father; but she has no authority over us." Nature was a solemn mother to the worshippers of Isis, "but Nature is not solemn to Francis of Assisi. To Francis, Nature is a sister, and even a younger sister: a little, dancing sister, to be laughed at as well as loved."

CARPE DIEM RELIGION

Mother Nature has not so subtle ways of making her point. I have passed the half century mark and with it has come, right on cue, a series of reminders. Mother Nature's chronometry is written into my cells, as if she wears a watch on her wrist for each of us that clocks the appearance of these reminders. There is the unintentional grunt that accompanies my otherwise graceful arising from a deep-seated chair. There is the fact that I can't sprint up a flight of stairs any more. There is the additional fact that I don't feel any desire to. I've begun to wear shirts that look like the shirts my father used to wear. There is that daylight savings time of life that turns back the hour of suppertime, bedtime, and wake-up. And the sight of gray has appeared in my mirror right on time.

Our youth-obsessed culture has about the same attitude toward a stray white hair as it has toward a stray mad dog, or a stain on the carpet. We are engaged in a battle against aging, and the white hair is like a white flag of surrender. So aging is something that must be cured. Aging is something we must be healed from. Aging is a pathology. What a strange concept.

Strange, but long-lived, and we are not the first to notice it. In the fourteenth century, a poet-philosopher named Francesco Petrarch wrote a script about an interior dialogue. He makes himself the dialogue partner of St. Augustine. The great Christian saint asks what Petrarch sees when he looks in the mirror. "Have you not noticed your face changing day by day and the traces of gray hair at your temples?" Petrarch replies that he expected a more profound question. Everyone sees traces of growing old, and he wonders what Augustine is getting at.

Augustine reveals it. "Tell me: when you noticed a change in some part of your physical appearance, did it cause a change in your soul?"

Petrarch mounts a defense. He has done his best not to be fearful, even consoling himself with great examples from history, like the emperor Domitian who said, "With a brave spirit I endure the sight of my hair turning gray in my youth." He wants Augustine to cut him some slack.

Augustine replies,

> I have nothing but praise for whatever causes you not to fear the onset of old age and not to hate it once it is upon you. But I have profound loathing and contempt for anything which tries to disguise the fact that old age is the point of departure from this life and says you must not think of death. It is a sign of a healthy disposition to bear calmly premature graying. But to stay the onset of old age, to subtract years from your age, to say that graying hair has come prematurely, to want to dye it or pluck it out, is the height of foolishness, though it is commonly done.

There was a strategy for not thinking about death that Chesterton noticed. "Many of the most brilliant intellects of our time have urged us to a self-conscious snatching at a rare delight." If we are all under the sentence of death "the only course is to enjoy exquisite moments simply for those moments' sake. The same lesson was taught by the very powerful and very desolate philosophy of Oscar Wilde." Chesterton refers to this as "*carpe diem* religion." *Carpe diem* may be taken positively to mean "seize the day" in the sense of not squandering it; but negatively and originally it meant to seize the pleasures of the moment without thought for the future.

This course of action is reputed to bring happiness, although it is more accurately named the "cult of the pessimistic pleasure-seeker. . . . The *carpe diem* religion is not the religion of happy people, but of very unhappy people." Joy does not come from deceiving ourselves about our mortality; from dying, plucking, and subtracting years; from trying to grasp the evanescent. "Great joy does not gather the rosebuds while it may; its eyes are fixed on the immortal rose which Dante saw. Great joy has in it the sense of immortality."

We should seize the (passing) day, but not for the sake of the receptacle. "It is true enough, of course, that a pungent happiness comes chiefly in certain passing moments; but it is not true that we should think of them as passing, or enjoy them simply for those moments' sake." Suppose one experiences a really splendid moment of pleasure.

A man may have, for instance, a moment of ecstasy in first love, or a moment of victory in battle. The lover enjoys the moment, but precisely not for the moment's sake. He enjoys it for the woman's sake, or his own sake. The warrior enjoys the moment, but not for the sake of the moment; he enjoys it for the sake of the flag. The cause which the flag stands for may be foolish and fleeting; the love may be calf-love, and last a week. But the patriot thinks of the flag as eternal; the lover thinks of his love as something that cannot end. These moments are filled with eternity; these moments are joyful because they do not seem momentary. Man cannot love mortal things. He can only love immortal things for an instant.

Chesterton would have us seize eternity, instead of the day.

KNOWING THE RULES

I think one of the most touching compliments ever paid to Chesterton is found in a letter written by Clare Nicholl, eldest daughter of the Nicholl family, which Gilbert and Frances encountered on a vacation trip, and who became almost a surrogate family in the following years. She wrote, simply, "he made one feel at home in the world."

I suppose it easy for any of us to remember some time, some place, when for some reason we did *not* feel at home, ranging from the first day of school, to attending a meeting for which our invitation was a mistake, to a dinner at which we did not know which fork to pick up. I submit that in such cases we feel the stranger because we don't know what is expected of us, and we do not know what is expected of us because we don't know what the rules are, and we do not know what the rules are because we don't know what game is being played. If through a misunderstanding we were to show up to a hockey rink in our roller blades, or bid six hearts in a hand of poker, or try to buy Boardwalk on the Parcheesi board, then we would not feel very much at home.

No place is homier than the nursery, and children like games there. "Children who are lucky enough to be left alone in the nursery invent not only whole games, but whole dramas and life-stories of their own; they invent secret languages; they create imaginary families; they laboriously conduct family magazines. This is the sort of creative spirit that we want in the modern world." But even nursery games have rules. The creative spirit operates in mimicry of cosmos, not chaos, and even nursery cosmology is ruled. Playing by the same rules is required in order to play with each other. The game would fall apart if a player trespassed the field's boundaries and tried to score a home run by sneaking through the bleachers, or another player snatched the ball from the scrimmage line to run for a touchdown while the opposing team was in a timeout on the sideline.

Chesterton could play—and laugh and chat and drink—with anyone because he thought everyone was in the game. No one was left out of the game. By the very fact of living, human beings have shared boundaries and a common field and a mutual purpose. In fact, the value Chesterton saw in a Church that was Catholic (the word means "universal"), quite apart from any supernatural claims, was its possession of a map of the human mind, a sort of rulebook, compiled from players who have dwelled in countless cultures and centuries. "It has been compiled from knowledge which, even considered as human knowledge, is quite without any human parallel. There is no other case of one continuous intelligent institution that has been thinking about thinking for two thousand years. Its experience naturally covers nearly all experiences; and especially nearly all errors." The Church has thought about the human game as it was played in the first century and the twenty-first, in Jerusalem or Paris or Timbuktu, and has drawn up a map of the playground "in which all the blind alleys and bad roads are clearly marked, all the ways that have been shown to be worthless by the best of all evidence: the evidence of those who have gone down them." If this institution also proffers doctrines and disciplines, it is only because the rulebook records what things have made the game go better. (I wonder if perhaps this is why Chesterton was not perturbed by authority: he saw the princes of the Church like referees in a game. If there are people who are playing the game, and people responsible for the rules of the game, there's no need for the former, who are having most of the fun, to be jealous of the latter even for their whistles and miters.)

Chesterton must have cherished Clare's compliment, too, for he observed that "Man has been a tramp ever since Eden; but he always knew, or thought he knew, what he was looking for. Every man has a house somewhere in the elaborate cosmos." The sorrow now is that for the first time, in a blinding hail of skepticism, he has begun "really to doubt the object of his wanderings on the earth. He has always lost his way; but now he has lost his address." Chesterton was a wonderful host at his home, or at any pub on Fleet Street, but Claire has expanded the compliment by expanding the environs. She says he has made her feel at home in the world. And if the whole world is now home for Claire, it must be because Chesterton has told her all the rules. Not one has been left out. He let her in on the game. "How can we contrive to be at once astonished at the world and yet at home in it? How can this queer cosmic town, with its many-legged citizens, with its monstrous and ancient lamps, how can this world give us at once the fascination of a strange town and the comfort and honour of being our own town?"

PLAYING BY THE RULES

Recently I persuaded my wife, just after I persuaded myself, that I needed a new PDA. (If you're unfamiliar with the jargon, that's a "personal digital assistant.") I didn't want it, mind you. "I needed it." I had been holding off replacing my first model, which was so old that it ran on coal instead of batteries, until I could afford one of the new models with a color screen. How many pads of paper and mechanical pencils I could have bought with the money I still finally spent, I do not know, but the PDA has one overwhelming advantage over pads of paper: you can download games into it. Not that this was the main reason I *needed* it, of course.

Solitaire is a pretty popular game for the PDA. Mine came already loaded with a version called Klondike, but there are other versions of solitaire and I reasoned that if I was going to use my PDA to its full potential, I should research this further on the web. First I found a program that played five versions of solitaire. Then I found one that advertised a dozen. Then I found a monster version with seventy solitaire games for the PDA, and a desktop version that boasted four hundred and twenty-two.

I am still in the trial mode of the software, and haven't decided whether to buy it yet, because I am overwhelmed by the rules. A Help Menu reveals seventy different sets of rules, containing phrases like, "Click to select two tableau cards whose ranks total to ten," and "Click to select cards of the same rank, regardless of suit; pairs are automatically discarded," and "Build down in alternating colors (for example, an 8C may be played on a 9D or 9H)." Rules account for how a mere fifty-two cards can yield four hundred and twenty-two games, or even the seventy at my fingertips. Rules achieve this multiplication of games by imposing limits on the player. In one game I am instructed that I may build up or down regardless of suit, while in the next I am sternly forbidden to lay a club on a spade. In one game I have the liberty of an autocrat to pair up cards of identical numerical value, while in the next, the very software itself rebels against me and refuses to lay one card on another if it is not both of an opposite color and a lesser value by one. Rules are nothing but limits.

Now, if it is true, as it seems to me, that freedom-loving Americans don't do very well with rules, and generally seek to avoid them, and usually try to get out from under them, then why don't the thousands of people who have downloaded this solitaire package feel oppressed by all these rules staring at them from the screen? Why haven't we risen up in rebellion and smashed our PDAs taunting us with rules? And yet, we don't. In fact, I could even imagine these libertarians returning the software if the only instruction in the Help menu was, "Put any card anywhere you want, until you win." How have we made peace with seventy sets of rules?

My guess is that when rules are limits, it awakens the gamesmanship of childhood. "It is plain on the face of the facts that the child is positively in love with limits. He uses his imagination to invent imaginary limits. The nurse and the governess have never told him that it is his moral duty to step on alternate paving-stones. He deliberately deprives this world of half its paving-stones, in order to exult in a challenge that he has offered to himself." (Just as the solitaire player deliberately deprives the deck of half the cards available to him by laying them face down.) Chesterton wrote those words in his autobiography, at age sixty-two, and went on to say "I played that kind of game with myself all over the mats and boards and carpets of the house; and, at the risk of being detained during His Majesty's pleasure, I will admit that I often play it still." He calls this the "game of self-limitation" and suggests that it is one of the secret pleasures of life.

Unlimited access to unlimited resources usually results in a bored, disaffected person. The surfeit of goods spoils enjoyment, usually. Pascal jotted, "It is not good to have too much liberty. It is not good to have all one wants." And this theme is sounded by most moralists who reflect on the vices and the virtues. They are not just being spoiled-sports or a nagging conscience. They know something about the cost of enjoyment. Something is not enjoyed unless it is loved; it is not loved unless it is precious; it is precious when it fills the eye of the beholder. Once this virtue is put into practice, then there is unlimited pleasure because the whole world fills our eye. "The charm of Robinson Crusoe is not in the fact that he could find his way to a remote island; but in the fact that he could not find any way of getting away from it. It is the fact which gives an intensive interest and excitement to all the things that he had with him on the island; the axe and the parrot and the guns and the little hoard of grain." It is a virtuous accomplishment to enjoy the game of self-limitation on our remote little celestial island floating through space.

A FINGER AND A FACE

Two years ago I committed one of the more heroic acts in my life. I drove in Italy. To locate my valor more precisely, I drove through Pisa to take my family to see "The Leaning Tower Of." Until that trip, my wife and children did not know my head could rotate so nimbly, or that a Fiat Punto could downshift from fourth to first gear at that rpm, or that the laws of physics could be flexed slightly in the cause of fitting in a parking space. Neither did I. So after ogling the sights, we rushed out of Pisa to avoid its real rush hour traffic, and retreated to our haven in Siena run by the Dominican sisters. Thus it was that I did not discover until it was too late—for nothing would induce me to a repeat automotive encounter with Pisa—that in our haste we had missed a remarkable sight. It is one I imagine many visitors overlooking if they are, as we were, distracted by the magnificent cathedral and baptistery and leaning bell tower. The university, I read in the guidebook, has one of Galileo's fingers.

At first the fact did not startle me, because after a week in Europe and visits to a number of churches, we had seen more bones than we do in America (in Minnesota, anyway). We had been to the Capuchin chapel in Rome ornamented with thousands of bones from their disrupted cemetery; we had worshiped in proximity with the bones of assorted bishops in numerous cathedrals; and on the hill above our hotel room in Siena, exposed in a side chapel of *San Domenico,* was the head of that city's most famous daughter, Catherine. But after a day or two, a theological divergence between the case of Galileo and Catherine began to appear in my mind. I could not keep from wondering how Galileo's finger was being preserved? Catherine's head was in a shrine, behind an altar. But since Galileo had been a university man, and his finger was at a university, I couldn't keep from remembering the formaldehyde jars in high school biology class that contained specimens of mice and jellyfish and baby rabbits. And the guide book made no mention of where the other nine fingers were to be found. Zealous medieval pilgrims sometimes stole relics; had Galileo's other fingers been translated to universities around the country by heliocentric devotees? And which finger was it? Possibly one capable of making a rude gesture at the inquisitors who had imprisoned him?

Most of all, I wondered what one could *do* with the finger of Galileo? Fingers usually point to things. Perhaps the finger was pointing to the sun as center of the universe, or to one of the four moons of Jupiter he discovered, or to a trenchant point in the theory of isochronism that he hypothesized at age nineteen. Fingers point, and whatever his bony finger was now pointing at, I was pretty sure it was still some part of the natural world that he had poked and prodded while he lived. On the other hand, what could one do with Catherine's head? Faces look, and sometimes when you look into a face you can see what the person is looking at. That's why although the Pope kept her body at Rome, he capitulated to a posthumous beheading so that Siena, and all pilgrims—medieval or modern—could look into her face once more. And I was pretty sure that Catherine was still looking at the supernatural world into which she had gazed while she lived.

Chesterton said, "The saint is a medicine because he is an antidote. Indeed that is why the saint is often a martyr; he is mistaken for a poison because he is an antidote. He will generally be found restoring the world to sanity by exaggerating whatever the world neglects, which is by no means always the same element in every age. Yet each generation seeks its saint by instinct; and he is not what the people want, but rather what the people need . . . Therefore it is the paradox of history that each generation is converted by the saint who contradicts it most." Galileo pointed out some marvels of this creation, but I'm not sure if they are as therapeutic to me as a woman who dialogued with God. Even if Galileo pointed to the highest heaven, a heaven beyond the range of his telescopes and ours, Catherine looked at something still higher, and pilgrims can see it in her face. Chesterton said it is the poet who asks to get his head into the heavens; it is the logician (and, I add, the scientist) who seeks to get the heavens into his head, and it is the latter's head that splits. Galileo had his finger trained on the sun to chart its course across the sky and prove we went round it, but Catherine turned her face to map our course to a yet higher reality. I do not say that Galileo's accomplishments are unimportant; I only say that I would not risk Pisa's traffic for anything he could point to, while I would join with other pilgrims in risking anything for that with which Catherine had come face to face. That's why we save her bones.

I COULDN'T CARE LESS

One often hears a person say, "I couldn't care less," and sometimes it is true. But there is a way to care even less than the person who says he doesn't care, and that would be indicated by not commenting on the fact at all. A nonconformist who prides himself on being free from material concerns might insistently protest "I couldn't care less about my pension fund," and he might be telling the truth. But a child of five is even more truthful by not making the statement at all. The child does not normally remark, "I couldn't care less about the impact the stock market is having on my IRA," because the impact of the stock market on IRAs is completely outside the consciousness of the child. One only comments upon those things that one is ready to notice, like water only pools where there is an indentation.

Under that principle, I wonder what it says about me that I have begun to comment upon—laughingly, of course, because I couldn't care less—the television commercials on the evening news. The same commercials appear night after night, and channel after channel, no matter how nimble is my surfing thumb on the remote. What a sad lot Madison Avenue must think the viewers are who tune in to the nightly news. The Nielsen ratings crystal ball must have divulged an army of anemic, allergy ridden, acid-refluxing persons with bronchitic windpipes, migrainous heads, arthritic joints, and overactive bladders. They are all desperate for advice that the medical establishment seems intent on withholding from them, because they are advised by the pharmacological industry to proactively seek out their doctors' counsel about a pill with a "Z" or "X" or "P" in its name to indicate strength, potency, and an exotic, magical quality usually associated with remedies coming from the Amazon rain forest. We do take our health seriously.

(It would be proper to pause here for a disclaimer and point out that there are people who do suffer, and that many pills do relieve suffering, and that I do not intend to make light of serious illness or appear ungrateful for medical resources, but I think I shall not do so. I will instead mimic Chesterton's high regard for the intelligence of the reader, who can reason out such a disclaimer for himself.)

Chesterton does not mind that we take health seriously, but he follows that very ancient and very Catholic principle that the seriousness of a thing is determined by taking the measure of the thing. This means that about man Chesterton is (a) more serious than those who put nothing under him, and (b) less serious than those who put nothing above him. Regarding the former, the philosopher who does not think a human being is any higher than the animals will not treat a person as seriously as Chesterton does; regarding the latter, the philosopher who does not believe there is a huge angelic world above human beings, not to mention God, will treat a person more seriously than Chesterton does. Knowing the correct placement of man in the cosmos affects the right estimate of man's needs. "In this matter, then, as in all the other matters treated in this book, our main conclusion is that it is a fundamental point of view, a philosophy or religion which is needed, and not any change in habit or social routine. . . . We need a right view of the human lot, a right view of the human society; and if we were living eagerly and angrily in the enthusiasm of those things, we should, *ipso facto*, be living simply in the genuine and spiritual sense."

Chesterton dealt with advertisements for health in his day, too. Dr. Gustav Jaeger claimed that we would be better off dressed in clothes made from animal hair, and drinking a milk protein called Plasmon that could ease the stomach by fully replacing the meat diet.

> And to those who talk to us with interfering eloquence about Jaeger and the pores of the skin, and about Plasmon and the coats of the stomach, at them shall only be hurled the words that are hurled at fops and gluttons, "Take no thought what ye shall eat or what ye shall drink, or wherewithal ye shall be clothed. For after all these things do the Gentiles seek. But seek first the kingdom of God and His righteousness, and all these things shall be added unto you." Those amazing words are not only extraordinarily good, practical politics; they are also superlatively good hygiene.

All things are put in proportion by taking their measure. "The one supreme way of making all those processes go right, the processes of health, and strength, and grace, and beauty, the one and only way of making certain of their accuracy, is to think about something else. If a man is bent on climbing into the seventh heaven, he may be quite easy about the pores of his skin." Chesterton thinks that what the modern world calls "taking thought" is properly understood as an act of rationalizing, and he agrees that some things should be pondered rationalistically. Care more about the kingdom of God, and you could care less about the commercials.

I DON'T SEE WHY IT HAS TO BE THAT WAY

once had a student in class whose every question over the entire semester always puzzled me. Whenever she raised her hand, I knew that I was not going to understand her clearly, that we were going to miss each other—like lines running on two different geometric planes. It would be an engagement between a whale and an elephant. And over the course of the semester I kept trying to figure out why this was, because I'm a rationalist who needs to account for things. Fortunately for me, the young woman gave me the key to solving the riddle in the second to the last week of class. It was a course in liturgical theology in which I had been explaining the movement from the Incarnation to the Church to the seven ritual sacraments. Her hand went up, and I inwardly sighed. I called upon her. She said, "I don't see why it has to be that way."

A little lit light bulb appeared above my head, the penny dropped, followed by the other shoe, and music of a revelatory kind began playing from the heavens. I had been explaining what was, and she was asking me *why* it was. I was describing a state of affairs, and she wanted evidence for why the affairs existed in such a state. What I was selling was not what she was shopping for.

It felt the same as if I had said, "So the man's sperm impregnates the woman's egg, and after nine months the baby is born," and she had given the same response: "I don't see why it has to be that way." What could I say? I don't know why it has to be that way, either. Maybe we could have been made in such a way that we could propagate by cutting off our little finger and growing a new baby, like the severed arm of a starfish can grow a new starfish, but there you have it. It isn't that way. All semester long I had been trying to describe how Christianity worked, and she was shopping for a persuasive, rational apologetic.

The experience got me reflecting upon two different kinds of explanation: the kind I was delivering, and the kind she wanted. One kind of explanation describes, explains, paints, exposes, connects, reveals and discloses. The other kind of explanation proves, tests, doubts, quizzes, disputes, argues and ascertains. One lives in the house, the other circles the perimeter. One explores from the inside out, the other wants to know if there are ways from the outside in, even if one is not planning to take the trip.

There was a time when I had greater sympathy for her kind of apologetics. I was a philosophy major; I liked logic; I thought Christian doctrine could be presented in a way that would cause the tumblers in another person's locked mind to click open. I laid systematic theology next to philosophy of religion and let them mate. But I confess that the process has lost some of its charm for me over the years.

I think this experience could shed light on Chesterton's method of proceeding in *Orthodoxy*. How many people have been converted either to Christianity or to Catholicism by that little book! It would make an interesting publication to gather together their essays about how the book had affected us. In a way, this is Chesterton's "apologetic" for Christianity, but it is an unusual one. He had published the book *Heretics* in which he expressed his dissatisfaction with the interior contradictions of various philosophies (better called "moods of the day") and someone pointed out that he had criticized other cosmic theories without giving his own. A certain Mr. Street wrote, "I will begin to worry about my philosophy when Mr. Chesterton has given us his." Chesterton smiled. And added, "It was perhaps an incautious suggestion to make to a person only too ready to write books upon the feeblest provocation."

But then he goes on to say that "I will not call it my philosophy; for I did not make it. God and humanity made it; and it made me."

In a sense, *Orthodoxy* can be read as his answer to "I don't see why it has to be that way." He says, "I don't know, either, but according to the doctrine of conditional joy keeping to one woman is a small price for so much as seeing one woman." "I don't know, either, but the Church has charted the paths that lead to dead-ends or to a swift fall over the edge of a precipice, and here's the map to the mind." "I don't know, either, but mysticism keeps men sane, and as long as you have mystery you have health." Or a hundred other lines snatched from the pages of this book would do.

Is it persuasive as an argument? No and yes. No, if you want to look at the question from a distance, consider it as a hypothetical abstract, glance at it and then plan to hear more of it later. Yes, if the shoe fits. But perhaps the riskiest quality is that if one accepts the description, one must submit to the agent describing. He concludes that he finally accepted the Church because "the thing has not merely told this truth or that truth, but has revealed itself as a truth-telling thing." It explains how things are, truthfully.

LIBERAL THINKING

I remember once being made uncomfortable about my occupation as a professor of theology. It was at a table of strangers at the reception dinner after a wedding, and the conversation began to unearth certain presuppositions that clashed with my profession. These fellow tablemates were civic activists who bicycled to work, recycled their newspapers, cleansed their colons, grew home herb gardens and ate organic tomatoes, worked their way through the New York Times' best sellers list on summer vacation, volunteered at the women's shelter, and walked for a cure for diabetes. What did I look like to them? Strike one: I was a professor. I taught instead of doing. Strike two: my subject matter was theology. I read books by dead white European males. Strike three: my area of focus was the liturgy. In this world of chaos and sorrow, I didn't light a candle to dispel the darkness, I read a book about candles that pious old ladies lit in the bowels of a cathedral that had taken money from the poor to build.

It was an uncomfortable reception dinner.

To this suspicious crowd I could have defended my hopelessly out-of-date irrelevancy by joking, as I sometimes have, that I read dead authors for the reason that I don't want to expend my time reading someone who is still alive, and might any day change his mind, and in his next book retract everything he has said so far. Under this principle, it is sad to note, but good fortune for me, that it is time for me to begin reading more by Stanley Jaki, who only recently died. (Actually, I could have begun reading him earlier, because he would not have changed his mind since he started writing, since he took a rather permanent view of things.)

The reason for this consistency of thought is revealed, I think, in an essay Jaki wrote entitled "Liberalism and Theology," in which he identifies liberalism. He defines it as "a habit of mind, a point of view, a way of looking at things." What is that spirit? He quotes Dorothy Thompson who said "liberalism is a kind of spirit and a sort of behavior, the basis of which is an enormous respect for personality."

By that, Jaki was not villainizing the liberal person, or the liberal cause, uncritically. He can acknowledge the liberal's capacity for justice, truthfulness, and self-command; liberals can be generous, open minded, and enterprising. But even so, Jaki says, "it is the essence of liberalism to focus on material well-being down here on earth." Of course liberalism will then work for justice and generosity: because we want well-being here on earth. However, the result (or cause) of this is an excessive focus upon the natural, and Jaki proceeds to work out the special emphasis on the natural over the supernatural in liberal approaches to creation, sin, Jesus, the sacraments, the priesthood, and more. "What is the common theological trait of all these manifestations of liberalism in theology? It is the upsetting of the balance between the natural and the supernatural."

After reading this, I thought of my dinner companions at the wedding reception once more, and concluded that "liberal" was precisely the right word to define them. They were reformers who worked for a good earth, and my study of a supernatural subject seemed to them childishly irrelevant. Jaki could describe them without ever having met them because he had met them a hundred times in other persons before. "Hence the emphasis of liberal theologians on respect, in the guise of ecological concern, for Nature as if Nature had been created for its own sake and not for man's sake." Save the planet, but we are not sure if we have souls to save, or if they need saving.

That something goes wrong when we upset the balance of nature and supernature was a constant refrain of Chesterton. "As a fact, men only become greedily and gloriously material about something spiritualistic. Take away the Nicene Creed and similar things, and you do some strange wrong to the sellers of sausages. Take away the supernatural, and what remains is the unnatural." Chesterton's conversion to Catholicism in no way involved a turning away from the world, or away from science, or away from the delights of nature. His conversion did involve finding a way to shoehorn the supernatural into the liberal's stubborn mind. I think that might be a way to describe the purpose of his book, *Heretics*.

This left Chesterton at an uncomfortable dinner once, early in his career. His tablemate at a Cambridge dinner abruptly turned to him and said, "Excuse my asking, Mr. Chesterton, of course I shall quite understand if you prefer not to answer, and I shan't think any the worse of it, you know, even if it's true. But I suppose I'm right in thinking you don't really believe in those things you're defending against Blatchford?" Chesterton says that he informed him adamantly that he most definitely did. "Oh, you do," he said, "I beg your pardon. Thank you. That's all I wanted to know." And Chesterton concludes, "He went on eating his (probably vegetarian) meal. But I was sure that for the rest of the evening, despite his calm, he felt as if he were sitting next to a fabulous griffin."

Imagine! A theologian who was a scientist, a scientist who believed in the supernatural—Jaki was a fabulous griffin himself.

HOMESICK AT HOME

E ven people who hold a casual acquaintance with Chesterton know him as a master of paradox. Now, paradoxes are easier to define than to explain, and easier to explain than to understand, so if we were to try to understand Chesterton's use of paradoxes it might behoove us to pick one out and study it. I have one in mind as a subject for study, a short one, a significant one because it was autobiographical, and one easy for us to understand at this particular moment. The paradox is: "one can be homesick at home." It is, as I pledged, short. It is also, as I said, autobiographical, coming from *Orthodoxy* where Chesterton wrote,

> I had often called myself an optimist, to avoid the too evident blasphemy of pessimism. But all the optimism of the age had been false and disheartening for this reason, that it had always been try-ing to prove that we fit in to the world. The Christian optimism is based on the fact that we do not fit in to the world. . . . I had been right in feeling all things as odd, for I myself was at once worse and better than all things. . . . The modern philosopher had told me again and again that I was in the right place, and I had still felt depressed even in acquiescence. But I heard that I was in the wrong place, and my soul sang for joy, like a bird in spring. I now knew why I could feel homesick at home.

And this is, as I promised, a propitious moment for us to understand it because many of us possess memories of a pang of homesickness.

My dictionary makes four efforts at defining paradox. It is "a seemingly contradictory statement that may nonetheless be true;" it exhibits "inexplicable or contradictory aspects;" it is "an assertion that is essentially self-contradictory;" or it is a "statement contrary to received opinion." Thus it would seem that the definition of paradox is based upon the idea of contradiction or contrariness or incompatibility. But why is this paradox instead of nonsense? Can words that are truly contradictory and incompatible be placed together meaningfully, say, for instance, "square triangle?" Isn't being homesick at home as nonsensical as being seasick in Nebraska or carsick in bed? Clearly we need to move from simple definition to explanation. Which brings me to my summer vacation.

Now, some readers may have thought, as I did, that with maturity comes a reprieve from the family vacation driving tour. But I discovered this past summer yet one more opportunity to cross half a continent and return in three weeks. A conference summoned me to California, and I persuaded my dean to give us gasoline for three instead of air fare for one. Over the course of three thousand miles I encountered a number of things that made me wish I was home—too firm motel pillows, mustard on sandwiches for five days in a row, freeways through prairie landscape, warm powdered lemonade, Los Angeles— but I would not say any of these caused true homesickness because there is something more to homesickness than a desire for comfort. Homesickness is the desire for home, and home is more than just the place where one is comfortable. Indeed, one doesn't long to be home because it is comfortable, rather home is comfortable because one belongs there. One belongs at home even when it's not comfortable, something that the breakup of the modern family indicates we have forgotten. But where do we belong?

To understand this paradox, we must know that Chesterton is asking this question not of particular individuals but of every human being. A particular person, such as myself, may be homesick in San Francisco, Yellowstone, or Los Angeles, because it is not my vocation to be a street car conductor, a park ranger, or a movie star. Were it so, then one of these could become home to me. So asking where we belong is another way of asking what is our task. Homesickness is an indicator of our vocation. On the one hand, we can accomplish our task anywhere, so we can be at home in any house or city or culture we have built. Chesterton is not suggesting we are homesick because this world is unpleasant (Lord knows how happy he was strolling into a pub anywhere on Fleet Street!). On the other hand—and this is the contradictory part of the paradox—he is suggesting that we were built for a longer-lasting happiness than any rest stop this world can offer. Our task is an eternal, spiritual one. It is the assignment of cooperating with grace to perfect our souls and attain complete beatitude. Such a task can be done anywhere—we carry it with us—and yet nowhere in this world will it be finished. We are at home anywhere in the world, but because we are eternal spirits we will remain homesick till the end. To understand Chesterton's paradox, one must know that he believes all human beings have within them a nature that directs them, like the swallows are directed to Capistrano, to the eternal, the ultimate, the absolute.